The Cop Doc's
Classic Writings on Police Reserves

Part of

The Cop Doc's Classic Writings
Series of Books

First Edition

Manufactured in the United States of America

ISBN: 978-0-9828697-2-7
(6X9 US trade paperback)

The information contained herein is not to be construed as legal, psychological, or other professional advice. Competent counsel should be sought from the appropriate professional.

www.TheCopDoc.com

The Cop Doc's
Classic Writings on Police Reserves

Part of

The Cop Doc's Classic Writings
Series of Books

By

Police Reserve Expert & Former Police Chief
Dr. Richard Weinblatt
The Cop Doc

Also by

Dr. Richard Weinblatt

Books

*Reserve Law Enforcement in the United States:
A National Study of State, County, and City Standards
Concerning the Training & Numbers of Non-full-time
Police and Sheriff's Personnel (1993)*

*The Cop Doc's Classic Writings on
Police Media Relations (2010)*

*The Cop Doc's Classic Writings on
Police Careers (2010)*

*Cops and College:
Lessons in Professionalism (2010)*

Also by

Dr. Richard Weinblatt

Columns

. Law and Order:
The Magazine for Police Management
"Reserve Reports"
(1991-2001)

Officer.com
"Reserve Power" and "Career Corner"
(2005-2006)

PoliceLink.com
"Law Enforcement Career Expert"
(2007-Present)

PoliceOne.com
"Weinblatt's Tips" and "Police and the Press"
(2004-Present)

Websites

www.PoliceReserveOfficer.com

www.PoliceChiefJobs411.com

About the Author

Dr. Richard Weinblatt, The Cop Doc, is a law enforcement expert, consultant, writer, radio show host, and media commentator, who has served as a police chief, criminal justice professor, and police academy director.

Dr. Weinblatt has worked in several regions of the United States in reserve and full-time sworn positions ranging from Auxiliary Police Lieutenant in New Jersey to Patrol Division Deputy Sheriff in New Mexico to Police Chief in North Carolina. A certified instructor for Taser, pepper spray, firearms, vehicle operations, and defensive tactics, he instructed and oversaw criminal justice degree programs and/or police academies in Florida, New Mexico, North Carolina, and Ohio.

With over two decades of concept research and practical experience regarding law enforcement reserves, Dr. Weinblatt is a sought after speaker and writer on the volunteer and part-time law enforcement officer topic.

He has authored several regular columns on reserves. Those include "Reserve Reports," which ran for a decade in *Law and Order: The Magazine for Police Management*, and "Reserve Power" for *Officer.com*. He wrote the *Reserve Law Enforcement in the United States* book.

Dr. Weinblatt is the former president of the Center for Reserve Law Enforcement, as well as the New Jersey Auxiliary Police Officers Association (NJAPOA – New Jersey's association for auxiliary and special law enforcement officers) which included its NJAPOA Training Academy and *The Shield* magazine. He is the creator of the website PoliceReserveOfficer.com.

Dr. Weinblatt is experienced with all facets of reserve operations. In addition to serving as a full-time law enforcer, he has served as a reservist on the street, a reserve administrator, a reserve liaison, and as a police chief who created and operated active police reserve and police explorer (for teenagers) programs.

A well-known police issues commentator for local and national media, Dr. Weinblatt has been interviewed by the Associated Press, CBS News, CNN, HLN, MSNBC, and The Washington Post among others. He has authored hundreds of articles on law enforcement topics for magazines and websites

Dr. Weinblatt earned a bachelor's degree in Administration of Justice, A Master of Public Administration in Criminal Justice, an Education Specialist degree, and a Doctor of Education.

Dr. Weinblatt resides in the greater Orlando, FL, area with his wife, Anne, and son, Michael. Further information is available at www.TheCopDoc.com and www.PoliceReserveOfficer.com.

Dedication

This book is dedicated to the men and women who for little or no money pin on a badge and believe in honor and integrity. They engage in a difficult profession to serve their community and advance forward when others retreat.

"The police are the public and the public are the police; the police being only members of the public who are paid to give full-time attention to the duties which are <u>incumbent on every citizen</u> in the interests of community welfare and existence."
- Sir Robert Peel, founder of modern policing

"You wouldn't go down (that alley) for a million bucks. A cop does it for a lot less. A Reserve does it for free."
- California Reserve Peace Officers Association

Acknowledgements

As with any author's book, many people are involved either directly or indirectly in helping the massive project come to fruition. This book was no different.

The genesis of the material for this particular book in The Cop Doc's Classic Writings series (as well as others in the series) came from the gurus, past and present, of the big law enforcement magazines and websites.

The list of them is long, but mention is certainly warranted of the following individuals that gave the green light to originally publishing these writings now given new life in the book series: American Police Beat's Cynthia Brown, Corrections Technology & Management's Tim Burke, Law and Order: The Magazine for Police Management's Bruce W. Cameron and Ed Sanow, Officer.com's Tim Dees, Police: The Law Enforcement Magazine's Randall C. Resch and Dennis Hall, PoliceLink.com's Chris Cosgriff, Kevin Powers, and Kendra Weikman, and PoliceOne.com's Scott Buhrmaster and Doug Wyllie.

Special attention is accorded to Bruce W. Cameron, the Editor Emeritus of Law and Order: The Magazine for Police Management, as he was the impetus for the writing endeavors back in 1989. My "Reserve Reports" column ran for ten years in Law and Order and had an incredible impact on volunteer and part-time law enforcement. That column wouldn't have been possible without Bruce Cameron who himself served as a reservist in Illinois and understood first hand its importance.

I also want to acknowledge the many reserve leaders who have put themselves out there, sometimes in the face of controversy, in a bid to advance the reserve cause. There are many that have contributed to this unsung corner of law enforcement.

It would be impossible to name all the reserve leaders and scholars that I have been in contact with over the past two decades. These are dedicated folks who have studied, championed, and worked towards reserve excellence. Among them are: David Blodgett, Daniel Brandt, Pat Feighery, Dr. Martin A. Greenberg, Erick Hoffman, Dr. Richard Kania, Terry Lattin, James C. Lombardi, Bill Martin, Mark Neeley, Barry E. Newman, David Rayburn, Frank Rizzo, Marc Spigel, and Brooke Webster.

While these trailblazers themselves have sometimes been controversial, there is no denying their respective contribution to the advancement of the reserve law enforcement cause.

Also of invaluable assistance was the family: Anne, the wifey, and Michael, the munchkin.

Contents

The Cop Doc's
Classic Writings on Police Reserves

Introduction

As a person who has been on both sides of the reserve law enforcement coin, I have been fortunate enough to be able to share information that I have learned with others who aspire to expand their knowledge concerning non-full-time law enforcement.

I have served as a reservist, an auxiliary program administrator, a reserve liaison, and as a police chief creating and overseeing a reserve program. Those experiences served me well as I have spent over 20 years living, studying, speaking, and being interviewed on this sometimes controversial and often misunderstood area of volunteer and part-time law enforcement that elicits a wide range of reactions.

For years I have answered questions and those queries have only intensified over time as community policing and budgetary constraints have become more prominent. What has remained constant for the police chief, sheriff, and law enforcers is the agency's mandate to provide quality public safety services to the community.

One of the main ways that I have been able to get the "word" and advice out to quench the thirst for information about the most misunderstood of professions is by having written hundreds of articles since 1989. In addition to articles on law enforcement reserve issues, I have also written on other police topics such as careers, tactical issues, media relations, and leadership.

I appreciate those many editors for their faith in my writing (and for their checks over the years so they could secure the first time publication rights). The articles have appeared in respected outlets including American Police Beat, Corrections Technology & Management, Law and Order: The Magazine for Police Management, Law Officer Magazine, Officer.com, PoliceOne.com, PoliceLink.com, Police: The Law Officer's Magazine, and Sheriff Magazine, among others.

The Cop Doc's Classic Writings on Police Reserves book is a compilation of articles on law enforcement reserve issues. It is part of a series of books sharing my classic writings on law enforcement topics. While the writings span over two decades, the information contained therein are as applicable today as when they were originally typed.

This book is designed to capture information that I had presented before in response to people's curiosity, but is no less valid in today's fiscally challenged world. If anything, I have seen the requests for reserve information ratchet up dramatically with the downturn in the economy.

The aim here is to help with the issues that span a broad police reserve spectrum. That includes the young man or woman who is contemplating how to successfully enter a career in law enforcement via a reservist stint, the community minded individual imbued with a passion for service to the nation in the post-9/11 era, and the full-time or part-time reserve administrator wondering what he or she should be doing to progress their unit forward. It also encompasses the veteran law enforcement executive contemplating the start-up, expansion, or re-vamping of a reserve or auxiliary outfit.

Indeed, many of the tips, suggestions, and concepts presented within these pages apply far beyond the scope of policing and extend into other areas of public and non-profit service, as well as the private sector.

It is my fervent hope that these timeless writings help you to reach your goals of reserve excellence and service to the community.

Some final thoughts…Volunteer and part-time law enforcement takes many shapes and goes by different names. Known variously as reserves, auxiliaries, specials, supernumeraries, intermittents, and other titles, please keep an open mind and remember that the training and duties may differ from another region's non-full-time law enforcers bearing the same title.

Additionally, while some of the facts and figures (such as basic training hours) may seem less than ideal by our standards today, please view them in the context of the date the information was gathered and the material was originally written.

Dr. Richard Weinblatt
The Cop Doc
Orlando, FL

www.TheCopDoc.com

Dr. Richard Weinblatt

Dr. Richard Weinblatt

February 1991
The Narc Officer Magazine

The Use of Reserve Officers in the War on Drugs

As the war on drugs continues, more and more criminal justice professionals are becoming aware of the vital role part-time, volunteer police officers fill. Commonly known as reserve or auxiliary officers, these unpaid men and women in (and sometimes out of) uniform are working with their full-time counterparts to take back their communities.

While the specific utilization of reserve officer resources may vary from jurisdiction to jurisdiction, all departments with active programs receive the benefit of a visible, uniformed deterrence. Some are even engaging them in investigatory details.

Mel Kalkowski, reserve captain and commander with the City of Anchorage Police Department in Alaska, said his reserves can discharge their monthly required hours "as desired."

Duties in Anchorage, in addition to highly visible road patrol, include assignments to vice and prostitution units.

The Harris County, Texas, reserve deputy sheriff's program goes even further. Some of the department's 360 reserves are used in actual undercover activities.

"The dealers know all the regular narcs," explained Chief Ray Vickers, reserve commander. "They even have pictures of them. The reserve can come in as an unknown."

Located in and around the nation's fourth largest metropolitan area, Houston, Vickers stressed that his reserves are trained thoroughly to enable them to handle the sometimes daunting task at hand. He said those reserves who desire to assist the Sheriff's Organized Crime Group (O.C.G.) get additional training. Participation in investigations is determined on a case by case basis.

"This is probably the most dangerous work a police officer does outside of traffic stops," said Vickers.

Agreeing that the approach has to be akin to a serious career activity, Kalkowski, who is studying for his master's degree in public administration, an interest in assisting the narcotics operatives is considered along with a hard look at the volunteer officer's experience, training, ability and the current need. Additional training is provided when appropriate.

Some departments use the reserves to supplement the regular force in areas where an occupational expertise is lacking. The Los Angeles County Sheriff's Department has an audio visual unit made up of Hollywood film wizards (reserves) which produces some of the slickest police anti-drug video presentations to come out of the law enforcement community (they also have great recruitment ads). Departments tap the talents of pharmacologists, lawyers, psychologists, public relations and advertising executives, and forensic scientists, among others.

Harris County's Vickers, a veteran of over 30 years of service, said one of his reserves had developed such an excellent talent for closing difficult drug fraud cases (involving pharmacists and doctors) that the D.E.A. reached out and hired him.

The Orange County, California, Sheriff utilizes reserves in his crime prevention section. They give lectures on the dangers of drugs. Also in California, Suzie Stutsman, with the Ukiah Police Department, was named 1989's reserve officer of the year in Ukiah for her many hours of volunteer work with the schools in the DARE (Drug Awareness Resistance Education) program. Stutsman has put in between 20-30 hours per week over the course of three years.

The most commonly thought of advantage in the utilization of reserve officers in the war against drugs is, of course, patrol. The high visibility marked patrol is the old standby of policing.

In New York City, the world's largest police department is emphasizing the use of auxiliary officers (they have 8,000 to pick from) on foot patrol in drug infested neighborhoods. Dr. Lee P. Brown, NYPD police commissioner and former chief law enforcement executive in Houston, Atlanta, and Oregon's Multnomah County, is pressing his community policing (CPOP) concept into the psyche of the agency.

The Baltimore County Police in Maryland routinely issues a "hot spots' sheet with locations their auxiliaries concentrate on.

"We'll certainly attempt to run the bad guys out of the area," said Don Stutman, auxiliary major of the organization comprised of some 125 volunteers. "However, our county does not contain the open drug dealing you might see in Washington, DC, or New York neighborhoods. Our marked units rolling through are the subtle hint which works best with our suburban users."

Stutman has the drug battle in his veins. The Baltimore lawyer is related to Bob Stutman, the legendary former head of the New York City office of the federal Drug Enforcement Administration (DEA).

The use of volunteer cops as part of the anti-drug effort has even taken route overseas. The Chief Commandant of the London Police's Metropolitan Special

Constabulary (England's top volunteer bobby), E.F. Maybanks, explained from New Scotland Yard that his 1,000+ men and women will soon be exposed to an expanded narcotics overview during their initial 6 month (on weekends) training period. They are already on the drug scene.

"We leave the investigatory work to the specialists, but there is no doubt we do impact on criminal activity with our presence," said Maybanks, a former regular officer whose daughter is herself a detective near Heathrow Airport.

Nowhere is the uniformed law agent's drug interdiction efforts more noticed, or dangerous, than in Florida. On the front lines of the battle are the 700 Auxiliary Troopers of the Florida Highway Patrol.

Harold L. Butterfield, Auxiliary Colonel, said his volunteer troopers run into most of the drugs during vehicle stops with paid troopers. He pointed with pride to the fact that no troopers have been killed in the line of duty while having an auxiliary with them.

"We've increased the auxiliary training to 18 weeks now with some time spent on narcotics matters" said Butterfield who has served the citizens of Florida for two decades.

Even the Florida Marine Patrol gets into the action with its small auxiliary contingent. Reserve officers with the Metro Dade County Police are well known for their thorough training when it comes to drugs.

Departments who have not yet utilized reserve or auxiliary officers in the fight against drugs are clearly wasting a valuable resource. The paid officer's effort against drugs only benefits with community involvement via the implementation of volunteer officer participation.

The reserve program must reflect comparable departmental standards of recruitment, selection, training and deployment. Clearly the paid officer cannot be successful in his anti-drug efforts alone. The officer needs a group of well-trained volunteers to tip the scale in our favor.

As one NYPD auxiliary police officer said as his uniformed presence temporarily halted business on a known drug transaction corner near Manhattan's Times Square: "We're all in this together."

Dr. Richard Weinblatt

Dr. Richard Weinblatt

May 1991
Arkansas Municipal Police Association Quarterly

Arkansas Volunteer Cops: A Vital Part of Modern Law Enforcement

Newport Police Chief Jerry Long was still getting comfortable in his newly acquired chief's chair when he emphatically declared his support for the eight volunteer officers who make up the Newport Police Auxiliary. Recently sworn in as chief in this Jackson County, Arkansas, town, the 18-year law enforcement veteran said in a telephone interview that his department's success with the auxiliaries greatly benefitted his community of 8,000 persons.

Such sentiments are in line with national trends indicating gravitation toward the use of modern police volunteers. As in Newport, municipal law enforcement volunteers (known as reserves or auxiliaries) in California, Texas, Florida, and other states are being recruited, screened and trained according to comparable full-time officer standards.

"Our auxiliary officers have uniforms and authority while on duty," said Chief Long citing a court decision requiring only radio supervision as sufficient to maintain the law enforcement reserve volunteers continuity of authority.

Bill Brown, Deputy Director of the Arkansas Commission on Law Enforcement Standards and Training, said auxiliary officers are required to receive 100 hours of training. Act 757 of 1983 establishes the statutory guidelines for the appointment and training of auxiliary officers who may not serve more than 20 hours per week.

Brown said the officers should receive the training which could be all 100 hours in the classroom or 40 hours in the classroom and 60 hours ride-along training.

Full-time officers in the State of Arkansas are required to undergo some 300 hours of training over the course of eight weeks.

No in-service training is required by the commission. However, "many departments set up their own required in-service training, including firearms requalification," said Brown.

While many cities in Arkansas do not yet have a reserve program, many are just being set up and have called upon Newport's 1-year-old program for guidance.

Lt. Bud Marshall of the Jonesboro Police Department was among those looking at established volunteer police programs to help them get a boost off the ground.

"We expect to have our 18 people rolling by the summer," said Lt. Marshall, who looked to Newport's exemplary volunteer contingent.

Lt. Marshall said his armed reserve officers will wear the same uniforms as the paid officers. Only the badge will differ from the one worn by the 59 regular officers in that the word "reserve" will be on it. There will not be a rank structure.

The Jonesboro P.D. reserves will break up their 16 hours of monthly on-duty patrol (8 hours), in a monthly meeting (4 hours), and in in-service training (4 hours).

Among the police departments not yet going down the reserve path are North Little Rock and Fayetteville. The Jackson County Sheriff's Office also does not have a volunteer deputy sheriff program in place.

The Little Rock Police Department has a 20-year-old program using auxiliary officers in non-sworn duties such as prevention and traffic control. They also ride as a second officer with a paid officer.

"Our volunteers are unarmed and serve in a support role," said Police Officer Bill Spencer speaking from the state capitol. "They do not have police powers."

Little Rock confines its membership to city residents. They undergo 60 hours of classroom training and 40 hours of field training (though it appears only two of the 12 are certified and must serve a minimum by the state due to the lack of enforcement responsibilities in Little Rock's volunteer program).

There are 12 auxiliaries in the department which is made up of 368 full-timers. One member was recently appointed the "Leader" to assist with the administration of the volunteer unit.

Newport's Chief Long said he views Little Rock's program as more of a cadet program.

"We used to have a cadet program and an explorer post, but discontinued them since we need more active assistance. Insurance also proved to be a problem," said Chief Long who said they were restricted to an eight member auxiliary due to insurance constraints.

Explorers are a "junior police" program run in cooperation with the Boy Scouts of America.

Capt. Clint Hutchins, of the Washington County Sheriff's Department in Fayetteville, said some of the Sheriff's Posse members are "as good as our regular people." He said the 32 volunteers wear the same exact uniform and undergo 100 hours of classroom training and on the job training. The agency, located on the Oklahoma border, is made up of 70 full-time deputies/jailers.

"Originally, they were a mounted riding club," said the former assistant chief of police with the Fayetteville Police Department. "We found they were of tremendous help, especially with manhunts in the rugged territory and mountains."

Differing in organizational strategy from the Newport P.D., which has a reserve lieutenant and two reserve sergeants, Capt. Hutchins said the Washington County Posse was incorporated on its own and had a "president, vice president, treasurer, and so forth. The Sheriff does have final say so on any subject."

"They do everything our regular people do. They just do it under supervision and for free."

Said Lt. Marshall: "We're looking forward to the good work our new reserves will do in Jonesboro. They will be a great help."

Dr. Richard Weinblatt

July 1991
The TMPA Quarterly
Texas Municipal Police Association

Texas Reserve Cops: The Lone Star State is Pioneering the Way

In the City of Bryan, Texas, the volunteer police reserve major and full-time owner of a real estate appraisal shop laughed as he recalled the roots of his volunteer law enforcement unit. J. Larry Locke, the volunteer commander, started his service in Bryan 25 years ago "…in khaki uniforms without a badge or gun and functioned as civil defense."

It's been a long road from those limited authority days of yesteryear for this city's dedicated cadre of reservists. The 24 current Bryan Police Reserves now sport uniforms identical (except for the slightly different badge and red epaulets on the shoulders) to the 70 full-time officers.

Reserve law enforcers in the state of Texas are a viable, growing phenomenon. According to Peter Stone, manager of public information for the Texas Commission on Law Enforcement Officer Standards and Education (TCLEOSE) based in the state capitol, Austin, there are (as of May 1, 1991) 5,669 armed, certified reserves in the state. Of those 2,890 serve as county reserve deputy sheriffs and 800 are county reserve deputy constables. The remaining 1,968 are with municipal police departments.

The assistant managing director of the Texas Reserve Law Officers Association, Bill Martin, a retired Dallas County reserve deputy sheriff, said his group has 3,200 members and that the reserve concept is spreading throughout the state like wildfire. While many departments, such as El Paso, Lubbock, Pasadena, Plano, San Angelo, and Waco, do not have active reserve units, sources indicate that other powerful agencies, such as Houston, are examining the concept and are expected to join the progressive trend, while still others have already successfully pioneered the increasingly traveled reserve program trail.

Reserves in Texas, who in other states are sometimes known as auxiliaries, receive their authority under three statutes in the local governmental code, Stone explained. Municipal reserves are featured under section 341.012. The municipality must pass an ordinance to form the police reserve. A county resolution passed by the county commissioner's court is necessary to for a sheriff's reserve (section 85.004) or a constable's reserve (section 86.012).

There are no state reserve troopers with the Texas Department of Public Safety.

Training

Stone said reserve appointees must be 21-years-old and meet training standards set by TCLEOSE.

"Before the reserve is allowed on the street in uniform, he must complete the reserve basic course consisting of 145 hours," said Stone. "The intermediate, 131-hour course is to be done within two years followed by the 124-hour advanced course within four years."

The three-step certification process equates to the 400-hour basic peace officer certification possessed by full-time officers.

Some departments, like the Bryan Police Department, have enacted even stricter guidelines for training. Reserve major Locke said his people undergo the full 400-hour Texas state certification training at one time. Locke said the training takes 11 months to complete going two nights per week.

"We want our people to get the training in one fell swoop," Locke said explaining why his agency has a stricter training time span requirement than even the already admirable standards of the state. "It's hard for a guy to keep ending and starting school over and over again."

In-service training is made available for reserve officers in much the same fashion as for their full-time counterparts.

"We've begun integrating reserve and regular training," said Captain David Torres, a 12-year veteran with the 377 member Corpus Christi Police Department serving a population of 302,000 people covering some 1,200 miles.

The enthusiastic reserve coordinator, who has filled the post for seven months, said the 29 reserves in Corpus Christi's program are given two to three months' notice prior to the in-service training held during daytime hours at the agency's in-house academy. They do not utilize a regional facility. He said most of the reserves are able to attend the day sessions on such topics as firearms, PR-24, and CPR.

Bryan's Locke takes a very strong stance on the in-service topic and said police reserve officers must attend a mandatory three-hour training meeting once a month. Officers who miss the session must serve the city of 50,000 population an additional five hours per month as a penalty if they do not have a valid excuse. Bryan's reserves each averaged a base of 21 hours of volunteer service per month last year.

"Some of our guys have been with us for 15 years, so they obviously do not mind the tough requirements," said Locke. Reserves short of hours are penalized at a rate multiplied by 1.25 hours. If their arrears fall to 32 hours, Locke said they are told to "turn their stuff in."

Uniforms

By and large uniforms for reserves mirror those of paid officers.

"Uniforms too distinctive from the regulars just confuse the issue and hurts morale. If the screening standards and training are similar, so too should be the uniform," said the Texas Reserve Law Officer's Association Martin from the group's Dallas headquarters.

As mentioned previously, Bryan's reserve uniforms are almost identical to those worn by regular municipal police officers.

Sherman Brodbeck, chief deputy and training coordinator for the Hays County Sheriff's Office, which patrols 720 square miles for a county population of 70,000, said his 25 reserve deputy sheriffs wear the same uniform as the 18 paid officers.

"The reserve deputies have a silver badge and the paid ones have gold ones," said Brodbeck.

Reserve deputy constables with the Harris County Pct. 1 Constables Office (there are eight elected constables in the county, each with his own geographic area or precinct), responsible for service of civil process and writs and subdivision contract law enforcement in the downtown area of Houston, have the same gold/silver badge setup as in Hays County. Captain J.H. Gilbert, the reserve coordinator over 38 reserves, also said that the color of the reserves' cap is different from the 92 paid deputy constables.

Our reserves end up spending around $2,500 of their own money as they buy their own uniforms and pay for the academy tuition," said Gilbert, who added that each reserve deputy constable must also secure a $2,000 bond.

On the other side of the Harris County law enforcement coin, the Sheriff's Department, responsible for the jail and for police services outside of the city limits, has its 380 reserve deputies appear in an identical fashion, according to Chief of Reserves L. Ray Vickers.

The uniform philosophy for the members of the Corpus Christi reserve is similar to those in the Dallas Police Reserve Battalion. According to reserve executive commander J.R. Crenshaw, City of Dallas Police reserve officers have the word "reserve" on their badge and patch. Corpus Christi volunteer cops also have "reserve" printed on their badge, but have "RES" in red letters on the shoulder patch.

Some Texas departments, in order to comply with regulations, are even placing the mandate "R"R on the back on the badge, indicating the extent to which departments are striving to have their reserve cops appear more and more identical to full-timers.

Reserve Advantages

Texas police administrators whose departments have successful volunteer officer programs all stressed the benefits derived by employing reserves. Reserves are discharging their required hours in a variety of different assignments which gives them ample exposure. The key is proper training and strong administration principles.

Reserves come from various walks of life and bring with them a unique perspective which oftentimes is advantageous to the agency.

Captain Gilbert said Harris County Pct. 1 Constable's reserves include a school board president, bank vice president, doctor and casket maker. Corpus Christi P.D.'s Captain Torres counts three morticians, as well as an accountant, office manager, and airline pilot among his reserve contingent.

"We couldn't function without them. They are a great amount of benefit to our department and play a great role in the law enforcement field," said Hays County's Brodbeck, a former reserve himself. He said they supplement the patrol aspect of his San Marcos-based department and have a mounted patrol unit which is utilized in parades, crime scene searches, missing persons, searches, and routine patrol.

"The reserves use their own horses and save us a lot of money. We coordinate some of the reserve patrols with the civilian block associations. It's also easier for us to evaluate candidates for full-time officers. We've seen them in action," said Brodbeck, adding that some reserves are in the Criminal Investigations Division (C.I.D.) doing crime analysis.

Captain Gilbert, with the Harris County Pct. 1 Constables Office, said that they also "save tax dollars by using the reserves as an applicant pool" while they serve the citizens of the county.

Reserve Major Locke said his Bryan outfit recently lost five reserves to full-time law enforcement positions.

"Because our application process and functions are the same as the regulars, our guys are great for full-time jobs. The five went to FBI, DPS, DEA pilot, a local narcotics task force, and a neighboring sheriff's department," Locke said proudly.

The volunteer commander of the Corpus Christi reserves, 10-year veteran and senior lead officer (which means she is solo-qualified) Loretta John, has carved an expertise niche for herself as a youthful gang investigator and is indicative of the creative ways that her agency is tapping the talent of young reserves. In addition to patrol, Captain Torres indicated that reserves in Texas' largest city south of San Antonio are also used as vice officers and traffic investigators. He said he wished he had started off as a police reserve as he "would have had a leg up coming on and known all the regular officers and how to do the job."

Conclusion

Reserve officers in Texas are clearly blazing the volunteer law enforcement trail. Successful programs share in common the elements of strong reserve administration practices and an agency chief executive who supports the concepts vigorously. Recruitment, screening, training and field training must be done at a level comparable to the full-time offices.

Dr. Richard Weinblatt

*October 1991
Law and Order:
The Magazine for Police Management*

The State of the State Reserve Trooper

Some volunteer law enforcement officers regularly cruise down the highways at speeds "slightly" higher than the posted limit. With their high beams on and urgent manner, motorists move ever so deftly out of the left lane. Who are these bastions of polished leather and mirrored sunglasses? Are they county reserve deputy sheriffs? Are they municipal auxiliary police officers?

If you guessed that the freeway fuzz is representative of the awe inspiring image and training that state cops embody, then you are correct.

A handful of jurisdictions employ volunteer officers on the state level. Arizona, Connecticut, Florida, New

Hampshire, New Mexico and Ohio are survivors in what was once a much larger, albeit exclusive fraternity.

All but Arizona have revamped their programs to more closely imitate the difficult application and training process of the full-timers. Arizona Highway Patrol reserves are already identical (except for the badge and paycheck) in every way to the regular state officers.

Extinct State Volunteers

The California Highway Patrol had auxiliaries in the early 1950s. According to Sgt. Greg Manuel, commander of CHP public affairs in Sacramento, the civil defense auxiliary was shut down for liability reasons once the Korean conflict had passed.

As detailed in the February 1989 issue of *The CHP Magazine*, published by the California Association of Highway Patrolmen, the 15 auxiliary members were not armed, wore a similar uniform (save for the auxiliary patch and hat emblems) and rode on regular patrols with full-time CHP officers. They even paid for their uniforms. Training emphasized radio procedures, first aid, traffic control, flare patterns, and firearms familiarization.

The Illinois State Police recently disbanded their reserve officer force which had been in existence for approximately 30 years. The concept never spread from its roots at the District IV. Station in southern Cook County/Chicago area.

According to an Illinois State Police sergeant who took part in the supervision of the civil defense charter-promulgated program, the dissolution took place after District IV.'s commander lost patience with the internal strife and political fighting within the volunteer unit.

Residency in the district, a cursory DMV and NCIC background check, and sponsorship by a full-time trooper made up the not quite so rigorous entry requirements. The Illinois sergeant, who wished to remain anonymous, said the 25 reserve troopers were not armed, but "had a similar shoulder patch and badge and undertook non-court related duties" during their eight hours of monthly service.

These factors, combined with training policies far below national volunteer officer standards (some first aid and a quick introduction to desk operations made up the minimal training standards) and Law Enforcement Accreditation considerations, led to the Illinois state reservists being left behind.

Nonetheless, for the remaining states, the charisma factor is high.

Trooper Aura

Harold L. Butterfield, auxiliary colonel of the Florida Highway Patrol, said some auxiliary troopers have left for local sheriffs' reserves only to come back to the fold eventually. The commander of the 700 member organization said those who return miss the higher level of prestige accorded to state cops.

Connecticut State Police Sergeant James J. Rodgers is the paid coordinator who rides herd on the 271 auxiliary trooper contingent. He agreed that the aura of the state police is a powerful drawing card. Rodgers' desk has been buried by a steady stream of applications which continue to pour in despite the moratorium forced by state budget difficulties. He hopes to start culling through the volunteer hopefuls in February of 1992.

"We've made the selection standards tougher," he said. "Outside of entry-level age requirements, the selection criteria, including mandatory Connecticut residency, is the same as is used for fulltime troopers."

Reserve Highway Patrol statewide reserve coordinator Sgt. Ivan T. Wooten, with the Arizona Department of Public Safety, said the sprawling geography of the state is the only factor which slows some people up in their eagerness to enlist. While the majority of his 57 reserves come from the Phoenix metropolitan area, due to the close proximity of screening and training locales, some 10 Arizona Law Enforcement Officer Advisory Council-accredited (ALEOAC) reserve academies dot the state, thereby ensuring easier access than might have been the case in years past.

He said his reserves, who must work 240 hours per annum, donated 20, 771 hours in calendar year 1990. Arizona's reserve officer screening standards are identical to those applied to paid state officers, as are Connecticut and Florida.

The selection process in Florida, previously conducted by auxiliaries, was taken over on January 1st by paid troopers. Said Aux. Col. Butterfield: "These guys do backgrounds all day. They know what to look for." Polygraphs, urinalysis, and other modern screening techniques have been stepped up in an effort to ensure that only the most qualified of applicants is eventually sworn in.

New Hampshire State Police Lt. Mark Furlone said the 31 auxiliary troopers in his agency go through an extensive background investigation similar to the 249 full-timers. The "Granite State's" auxiliary troopers, who carry Smith & Wesson 5906 .9mm firearms, only have arrest powers while on duty. They must possess a valid New Hampshire driver's license, reside in one of the six field troops and be at least 21 years of age.

Lt. Furlone said the State Police provide all equipment with the exception of a bulletproof vest which is mandatory. Auxiliary uniforms are identical including the badge. The only difference manifests itself in the form of a rocker under the shoulder patch which says "auxiliary." The ID card states "auxiliary" as well.

In New Mexico, the state volunteers are the descendants of a mounted posse formed by the governor in the 1930s. No longer content with the sole qualifications of possessing a horse, saddle and rifle, the modern day New Mexico State Police have established a demanding, symbiotic relationship with the 50-year-old organization, which, in an unusual statutory set up, is technically a separate state law enforcement agency.

Applicants are subject to an oral review board, NCIC background check and random drug screening. Much like the Royal Canadian Mounted Police, New Mexico's Mounted Patrol is no longer confined to horseback and more often utilizes marked police cars.

"The name is a misnomer," NMSP Major Frank Taylor, the paid liaison, said. The agency has 300 armed volunteer officers who patrol in pairs in their own marked units or as a passenger in a regular cruiser with a full-time New Mexico State Police officer.

Members are allowed to use their own vehicles (free Mounted Patrol official license plates are furnished) provided the car meets inspection criteria involving emergency lights, siren, two way radio, first aid equipment and magnetic door signs. They do sometimes ride horses for crowd control or search and rescue assignments. They have police powers while on duty.

The Ohio State Highway Patrol just put their program though a major overhaul. "Our auxiliary program is support oriented," Captain Howard Shearer said. He explained that the 141 auxiliary troopers ride as shotgun officer with one of the 1,249 uniformed personnel.

The volunteer candidates, who must be 21 years of age or older and a resident of Ohio, are subjected to a background check handled by the auxiliaries.

Trooper Training

Once a candidate is sworn in, the fun really begins. Training for the state outfits is rigorous, mirroring the challenges experienced by the full timers.

In Arizona, easily one of the most advanced reserve states in the nation, reserve officers with the highway patrol must complete 440 hours of training, over the course of a year, pursuant to ALEOAC standards. 320 hours of field training has to be completed within one year of graduation and eight hours of advanced training per annum is required to maintain certification.

Florida, unlike the other states which use the terms reserve and auxiliary to connote basically the same function, has two distinct statutory levels of law enforcement volunteers. The Florida Highway Patrol uses both designations which are screened identically to regular troopers. Only the training and type of duty differ for the 700 auxiliaries.

FHP reserve troopers, of which there are nine, undergo the same exact Florida Division of Criminal Justice Standards and Training certification (620 hours) full-time police officers are subject to. Reserve troopers, whose part-time trainings schedule takes over a year to complete, have the same authority as the 1,644 paid troopers and are able to work the highways alone.

Aux. Col. Butterfield, who has spent seven years as the volunteer commander, said his auxiliaries undergo 124 hours of training by FHP troopers. They must discharge their required service of 24 hours a quarter alongside a fully certified officer. Training generally takes place in four to eight hour sessions with scheduling decisions made at the local troop level. Firing range time is extensive.

Like Arizona, the FHP allows prospective volunteers to take the training at their own expense at certified community colleges. However, if they choose to train at a non-FHP facility, reserve and auxiliary troopers must re-qualify with their firearm for a Florida Highway Patrol rangemaster and must complete an FHP orientation course.

New Hampshire auxiliary troopers meet the same training requirements set for all volunteer or part-time officers in the state. Two training schedule options are available. "Option one involves ten weekends of training and option two involves two weeks of full-time training which takes place in the summer," said Lt. Furlone, commander of the Special Services Unit, which oversees the auxiliary trooper program.

New Mexico Mounted Patrol Training Sgt. Frank R. Kosciow explained that the 300 volunteers who assist the New Mexico State Police undergo 200 hours of combined training made up of a pre-commission phase and a post-commission component.

"Pre-commission officers can work unarmed in cadet fatigues under the direct supervision of a mounted patrolman or state police officer. When they are commissioned, they can carry and act as mounted patrolman provided they complete the more advanced post-commission training within a year," Kosciow explained (he is a volunteer who is an academy-certified police instructor). He added that they must pass a police officer proficiency exam (POPE) at the end of each stage and also go through a formal 100 hour field training program.

The 141 auxiliary troopers in Ohio have a newly upgraded training mandate of 82 hours with the scheduling handled at the nine out of ten total districts which are involved in the program which was founded in 1942.

In-service training in New Mexico is just like that of the full-time troopers with requirements in place for 20 hours per year to be completed.

Butterfield said FHP auxiliary in-service training must be taken at the rate of 12 hours per year with the majority of the auxiliary troopers attending the annual training seminar to satisfy the policy.

The members of the Connecticut State Police's auxiliary program, which has been in existence since 1941, used to undergo 100 hours of training one night a week for 26 weeks. Sgt. Rodgers said the new policies will raise the next bunch of auxiliary recruits' training to 207 hours with 24 hours devoted to firearms sessions.

All of the officials interviewed declared a resolve to push their volunteer state troopers forward into the '90s with broader responsibilities and more sophisticated training.

Taylor and Kosciow both said that they too are looking at improving New Mexico's already solid program. New Mexico's aggressive concept already takes their volunteer troopers into all facets of law enforcement. Mounted patrolmen handle a broad spectrum of assignments including accident investigation and undercover narcotics work with the Special Investigations Division (SID).

"Our people are dedicated and are always looking for new challenges," Butterfield said of his Florida Highway Patrol volunteers who donate an average of a quarter million hours each year. He said that some individuals personally contribute 2,000 hours annually.

"We're committed to having the best auxiliary troopers we can," Rodgers said.

Dr. Richard Weinblatt

October 1992
Law and Order:
The Magazine for Police Management

Reserve K-9

A recent stolen car chase and subsequent suspect flight on foot was resolved due to the involvement of Flat Rock, MI, K-9 Auxiliary Police Officer Steven M. Kulakowsky and his partner, a four-year-old American German Shepherd named Chester the Arrester.

"Chester unfortunately got his leg caught jumping over a guard rail," related the human half of the three year old partnership based some 30 miles south of Detroit. "But he wanted to continue tracking and caught the suspect in a field."

Four pins in his leg later, Chester, who has sniffed out $100,000 from 15 vehicles, is slated to go back in service shortly. Personally saddled with hefty surgical bills, volunteer officer Kulalowsky said the assistance he received from full-time officers in the area is a testament to the good work Chester has done. Officers with departments in the Down River Area Police Association, which shares resources among each other on a mutual aid basis, contributed money to pay for Chester's medical bills.

It's a team effort here. That's why we're so successful. The dog goes places where others wouldn't and is appreciated by the officers," beamed a proud Kulakowsky.

The national trend which has integrated volunteer and part-time officers in specialized aspects of modern law enforcement is also present in canine units where both dog and handler work for little or no compensation. In fact, many officers, such as Kulakowsky, personally pay for the necessary equipment in order to stake out an unusual parcel of reserve turf.

Reserve canine units reflect the different operational philosophies and take on the variety of diverse characteristics and traits just as their full-time counterparts do. Some K-9 teams are cross-trained for the plethora of different tasks needed- patrol, narcotics, search and rescue or bomb sniffing- while others possess only one skill area.

In Southern California, law enforcement agencies throughout the region have come to rely on a team of six reserve deputies out of the Orange County Sheriff's Reserve Forces Bureau. They and their bloodhounds worked approximately 10,000 hours last year.

The only bloodhound team in the area, Reserve Lieutenant Lawrence R. Harris, a fully certified California Level I. reserve who serves as the unit's commander, said the watch commander has the authority to send a dog unit out. They can be on scene anywhere in the 786 square mile county within an hour. Harris said the benefits are there for the 1,276 full-time deputy department to have a K-9 reserve program.

Harris, who has volunteered as a reserve for over 30 years with the California Department of Fish and Game, the Newport Beach Police, and now the Orange County Sheriff, said he revitalized the bloodhound program six years ago when he transferred to search and rescue. The previous program had fallen apart and, according to Sergeant Richard A. White, the coordinator who oversees all 260 reserve deputies for the department, Harris "ran with it and has done a great job."

Harris enlisted his wife, a Newport Beach Police reserve officer, in the training of the bloodhound puppies. "We started to train daily and now are at three times a week," said Harris who partners with two female bloodhounds, Sable, age 5 ½, and a four-year-old named Duchess. They are cross-trained for searches of people and cadavers on land or water. "They can trail on a boat or from the shore.

Kulakowsky, whose municipality encompasses 30,000 people in 13 square miles, said he started three years ago after watching a friend train dogs for guard work. "I took bite hits, laid down tracks, and helped him with the training. When I had the chance to get a puppy, I thought why not do this myself," he said.

Kulakowsky explained that, prior to his involvement, the only K-9 units available were from the Michigan State Police. Much like what has happened in Orange County, CA, since the inception of the sheriff's reserve K-9 program, departments in the vicinity of Flat Rock enjoy a quick response to their call for a dog unit.

"We do a lot of public relations for the agencies also. A lot of the small cities nearby such as Riverview call on us for school demos," Kulakowsky said.

Kulakowsky and Chester underwent an intensive training period of eight months before being certified by the Cumberland, IN, National Police Work Dog Association and hitting the streets.

"Chester is a full service K-9 in seven areas," Kulakowsky said. "He can do narcotics, both suitcases and building types of searches, tracking, articles, search, area search, and aggression control. My dog is not trained on immediate bite. He bites only on command."

Harris said his bloodhounds bite "only the food which is fed to them."

Similar to paid counterparts, Kulakowsky echoed Harris' comments stressing the importance of the bond which forms between man and dog thus enabling the handlers to "read the dog and establish P.C. (probable cause)." Both agencies have the dogs live home with their handler.

In Orange County, the department owns the dogs and provides the vehicles and equipment needed. "I have a fully marked sheriff's Dodge Supervan in my driveway with kennels and all self-sustaining equipment, as well as the lightbar, radios, siren, shotgun and other equipment standard in cruisers," Harris said.

He added that all vet bills are sent directly to the agency. "A pet food company donates about $2,200 worth of dog food to the unit per year."

Kulakowsky has personally paid for his training (not to mention time off from work) including a recent week-long trip to Fort Wayne, IN. He even paid for his response vehicle, a Ramcharger loaded with authorized police equipment including emergency strobe lights in the grill, siren, and two-way radio. The vehicle says "K-9 Unit" on the back.

When he first got involved, the city didn't pay for anything, Kulakowsky said, but now they pay for a lot of things including gas and lodging.

Kulakowsky, who wears a special SWAT-style dark fatigue uniform and carries a Glock 9mm Model 17 on duty, explained that the department signed a contract which clarifies the placement of liability upon Flat Rock. "They assume all the liability and court costs and cover the K-9 vehicle," he said. He owns Chester personally and has insured him to the tune of $6,000.

Reserve K-9 units are on the rise, as is reserve law enforcement in general, reflecting the professionalism and training pervading the citizen cops ranks. "You can only hunt once a year in the traditional hunter role," Orange County's Harris said, reflecting on the challenges this unique area of reserve policing provides him and his handler colleagues. "With the dogs, you can hunt all year round."

Dr. Richard Weinblatt

Dr. Richard Weinblatt

December 1992
Law and Order:
The Magazine for Police Management

Reserve Wildlife Officers: A Different Breed

When a reserve deputy with the Sheriff's Office of Cocino County, AZ, was killed in the Flagstaff area by a suspect with an AK 47, Lawrence S. Mayer's wife felt the stress of having a law enforcement officer for a husband. The situation was made even more chilling due to the fact that the reserve deputy, like Mayer, was a physician who volunteers to patrol some of the most remote areas of the Grand Canyon state.

Mayer, aside from his status as a highly credentialed college professor sporting M.D. and Ph.D. degrees, is a different breed among the nation's quarter of a million reserve officers. He finds challenges in his reserve game ranger role with the Arizona Game and Fish Department. Mayer and other state reserve wildlife and conservation officers routinely confront people in sparsely populated areas who are carrying high powered weapons and, more often than not, are drinking.

While volunteer and part-time law enforcers (known in various jurisdictions by many titles including reserve, auxiliary, or special) have become widely known in municipal police and county sheriff's agencies, a handful of states utilize them in statewide wildlife law enforcement operations. Not to be confused with the eight states which have volunteer state troopers in their state police/highway patrols (Alabama, Arizona, Connecticut, Florida, New Hampshire, New Mexico, Ohio and Vermont), reserve game wardens have quietly evolved to a highly sophisticated and professional level in such geographically diverse states as Arizona, California, Florida and New Jersey.

"We even have full-time officers who want to serve part-time in the great outdoors," said Donald M. Turner, field operations coordinator for the Arizona Game and Fish Department which has 25 reserve game rangers from all branches of life. He said a whopping 70% are full-time police officers with other agencies.

"Some eventually leave after discovering they're not comfortable having their closest backup two to three hours away." Turner pointed out that his people, whose average patrol district is 1,400 square miles, were nine times more likely than other law enforcement personnel to be killed due to the factors mentioned such as the presence of rifles.

Lt. Mike Boyle, training officer for the New Jersey Division of Fish and Game, explained that a section of state law Title 23 enables the Division to appoint deputies, and that the "nature of the job is relatively dangerous." The division currently boasts 90 trained, Glock .9mm toting deputy conservation officers, throughout New Jersey, continuing a program which started in 1895. As elsewhere, some are full-time law enforcers with a yearning for the great outdoors.

Boyle said that they've held several training courses for candidate deputies and that each class has seen the training hours increased. Some 700 inquiries were received the last time around.

Another crop of conservation officer deputies is slated to be harvested after the first of the year via a 200 hour course covering search and seizure, patrol, first aid, defensive tactics, wildlife law and 48 hours of firearms. Classroom facilities are in Freehold Township, and tactical and range activities takes place at a second site in Jackson Township during the 10-month weekend course.

"We're interested in people who have a sportsman's level of knowledge," Boyle said. He added that the person's place of residence is compared with the area's need for deputy conservation officers. He said, for example, that the Burlington County area is in need of volunteer deputies whereas the counties of Camden and Gloucester are not.

According to Boyle, interested individuals are encouraged to send a letter detailing why they would like to be appointed deputy conservation officers. Following a review of the letter and geographically related deputy manpower needs, applications are sent out. Two interviews, a background investigation and a written exam are held, as well as a physical exam at the applicant's expense. During the initial training phase, trainees undergo psychologicals and urinalysis which are administered by the state of New Jersey.

Boyle said the uniform and firearm costs, which come to about $2,000, are borne by the deputy conservation officer. The only difference in the uniform manifests itself in a "deputy" tab on the badge. He explained that deputy conservation officers work "under the supervision of a regular officer 90% of the time enforcing wildlife laws."

Auxiliary wildlife officers with the Florida Game and Fresh Water Fish Commission, like the other states' game wardens, may themselves be serving full-time as a municipal or county law enforcer.

Florida's version requires that the volunteer be certified at either the 120 hour auxiliary or 520 hour part-time/reserve officer level set forth by the Florida Criminal Justice Standards and Training Commission. In a slight twist from what occurs elsewhere in the state, however, volunteer wildlife officers regardless of their level of training are all titled "auxiliary" with no visible distinction.

Most of the Florida's several hundred auxiliary wildlife officers, who qualify with their firearm twice a year, have taken training through a local community college, though every few years the Game and Fresh Water Fish Commission itself sponsors an academy. All training, uniform, firearm and equipment costs are carried by the auxiliary. Interested candidates fill out an application, undergo a background check, and must pass a four person interview board.

Reserve fish and game wardens with the California Department of Fish and Game's Wildlife Protection Division find their way into service by being sponsored individually by a full-time warden. Michael A. Grima, the deputy chief over such critical domains as hiring and training for the agency, said that wardens work independently from their homes to cover their vast beats. "The reserve and the full-time wardens have to work closely together for a minimum of 16 hours per month. That is why reserve must be approved and sponsored (by a full-timer) and why there is no need for a formal probation period."

Grima, who holds a bachelor's degree in wildlife management, said that "a full gamut of folks who enjoy the outdoors have applied and become reserves including a deputy district attorney." He said the reserves pay for their own uniforms, firearm and gear. The agency issues a check for $100 each year to defray the cost of uniform cleaning and also pays reserves' travel and per diem costs.

Grima's 370 full-time wardens are backed by 75 identically uniformed, save for the badge which reads "deputy." California Commission of Peace Officer Standards and Training (POST)-certified reserves. The 13-year law enforcement veteran said 35 are non-designated Level I. reserves and the remaining 40 are Level III.s.

Under California regulations, non-designated Level I. reserves undergo a minimum of 640 hours of training and are allowed to perform general law enforcement duties solo while on duty. Level III. reserves receive a minimum of 56 hours of training, including firearms, and do initiate independent law enforcement action. A Level III. reserve warden works with a Level I. reserve or a full-time fish and game warden.

"We have Level III.s control suspects, inventory evidence and patrol as a second officer," Grima said. He has served as deputy chief for one year overseeing the –ten-year-old reserve program. "Full-time wardens undergo 20 weeks (five months) of training from 8:00 am to 5:00 pm. Most of our reserves take the Level I. or III. course at a community college at night or on the weekends, though five reserves have gone through the full-time academy."

Academy training in Arizona's certification program encompasses just one type of officer: the full 440 hour Arizona Law Enforcement Office Advisory Counceil (ALEOAC) certification. After progressing through a series of hurdles, including an interview panel and criminal history check, the candidate is sponsored through one of the community college academies, which costs the volunteer ranger hopeful over $1,000. They must also pass a written exam.

Arizona reserve game ranger Mayer, who was a volunteer deputy warden in California, said it took him 12 months to complete the ALEOAC training at Mesa Community College in Mesa, AZ. "We went two nights a week, all day Saturday and all day for half the Sundays," he said.

"Arizona reserve game rangers work by themselves, are covered under workman's compensation, and carry a gun 24 hours a day, seven days a week," Turner said. They are granted permanent status after one year's probation. "There is no difference between them and paid rangers, and we have a policy not to indicate reserve status. Their badge and ID 9card) is the same. They are full peace officers and often back up deputy sheriffs and highway patrol officers in remote areas."

"Some of our guys go all out and purchase all of the items on the field operations supply and equipment list. Since they may be out for a few days at a time, they use the stuff," Turner said.

At a minimum, the reserve is responsible for buying the $1,500 specified uniform and a Sig Sauer .45 or .9mm firearm. The Sig P230 is the optional but officially approved backup gun. The Arizona Game and Fish Department provides badges, shoulder patches, name plates and two ID cards for the 25 part-time reserves, some of whom ride horses on patrol.

Reserves attend a three week Post-Academy course during the day, necessitating the volunteer take time off from his or her full-time occupation. A 100 hour field training officer (FTO) program must also be completed.

In order to maintain certification, 48 hours of service must be rendered semi-annually. The reserve game ranger has to undergo eight hours of state required advanced officer training, any internal training mandated by the department, as well as qualify on the department course four times a year and the state course once a year.

Mayer, who has put in as much as 1,000 hours a year for the state of Arizona, said he enjoys the law enforcement aspects of being a reserve game ranger and recently has begun patrolling a lake on a bike. "This is just a tremendous experience."

Dr. Richard Weinblatt

Dr. Richard Weinblatt

Spring 1993
The F.O.P. Journal

Reserve Policing: Stepping Stone to a Career

Ryan T. Kane views his work as an auxiliary police officer in South Brunswick Township, NJ, as more than just a sideline activity. The 20-year-old criminal justice student is actively experiencing, through his volunteer law enforcer stints, what his future might look like as a full-time officer.

"We expect to have about eight auxiliaries apply for our openings," said South Brunswick Police Captain Frederick A. Thompson. The holder of a master's degree, Thompson, like other progressive police executives, has identified in-house reserve forces as a testing ground of sorts for future full-time employees.

Kane, who is a certified Monadnock PR-24 sidehanlde baton instructor, represents one of the two large segments that make up the nation's 250,000 reserve law enforcement component. Volunteer or part-time police officers have long used their service as a stepping stone reflective of their career aspirations. The other segment of reservists is successful members of the community who give back to society through their service.

Sometimes called auxiliary or special officers, reserves in most jurisdictions have to overcome similar or identical screening and training challenges as those confronting regular officers. Many have had the same state certifications as full-timers and cross over to salaried status without having to go back through a police academy again.

Many administrators gravitate to the concept as it allows them to see how prospective officers react, sometimes quite literally under fire. "We encourage our auxiliaries to pursue a career. We know what they can do as we've watched them in action in uniform already," Thompson said.

Providing the basis of any good reserve springboard is a bona fide police training regime. Reserves in North Carolina must meet the same minimum training standards and thus find themselves using their certification when they go full-time. In the Tar Heel State, reserve and full-time deputy sheriffs undergo 444 hours of academy training whereas reserve and full-time police officers get 432 hours. The distinction is made police versus sheriff; not reserve status as opposed to salaried occupation.

In a similar vein, the Georgia Peace Officer Standards and Training Council's Jim Sims said that their attorney general has said, "If it walks like a duck, it must be a duck." The state makes no distinction between paid, part-time or volunteer officers provided they are 280-hour fully POST certified.

In the shadow of New York City, special police officers in Greenwich, CT, also go through an identical screening and training process. The training is the standardized 498 hour Connecticut Municipal Police Training Council (CMPTC) mandated curriculum. The difference manifests itself only in the scheduling as the training is conducted at night and on the weekends for a longer period of time.

The convenience of an identical academy scheduled for reserves does not go unnoticed by salaried personnel. In Memphis, TN, the current 430-hour Shelby County Sheriff's Office Reserve Academy, identical to the full-time day academy, boasts 16 newly minted regular law enforcers as students.

Chief B.J. Patterson, director of the reserve deputy sheriff program, said the uniforms, badges and identification cards are identical for the reserves. It makes sense to them that the training is on an equal par and is therefore attractive to all facets of law enforcement.

The Ramsey County, MN Sheriff's Department takes the concept of reserve to full-time one step further. The reserve program, based out of their Shoreview offices, is mostly comprised of criminal justice students who are using their service as a stepping stone into a full-time career. Of the 70 reserves, 40 have earned their 400-hour Minnesota- state license and are therefore carrying Glock Model 17 firearms and are solo qualified. The remaining 30 non-licensed reserve deputies must have 36 hours of pre-service training and they patrol unarmed under the watchful eyes of a certified officer. Once again, the entry standards are rigorous, mirroring the full-time standards, and include MMPI psychological testing, and drug screening.

"We go through the same training and are fully state-certified police officers," said Special Sergeant Eric Omdahl, Greenwich's top volunteer cop, who added that his officers have the legal right to carry firearms off duty.

Departments from Anchorage to Honolulu utilize the same entrance standards for reserves as they do for full timers. In most cases, the screening elements include a written test, background investigation, oral interview, psychological testing, physical agility test, medical exam, drug urinalysis and a polygraph test.

Over in Boise, ID, one of the nation's fastest growing regions, Jim Fox, the deputy sheriff who oversees the Ada County Sheriff's Office's Reserve Deputy Program, said their biggest problem is the exodus of volunteers to full-time law enforcement slots. "We screen these people as we do for regular deputies," explained Fox. "They have to go through a written test, oral interview, physical assessment and final interview."

Once past the entrance and training phases, the experience gained though actual work in the field proves invaluable to aspiring full-timers. Becoming a working reserve allows the young adult to separate fact from fiction often portrayed on television. Being a police officer becomes real.

"Someone who has worked for us as an auxiliary officer and is experienced knows this is the career for them," said Thompson.

The experience South Brunswick's Kane has garnered through his service as a volunteer police officer has not only given administrators a peek at his abilities, but has also given him an insight into himself. "After being involved in my first foot chase, I feel confident I can do the job," said Kane recalling one of many eventful evenings on patrol. In-service training ensures that the reservists stay up on the latest police procedures and equipment. Theories and intangible concepts become concrete when merged with the sights and sounds of the streets of justice.

Ada County requires that eight hours be spent on in-service training each month. The figure does not include patrol or other reserve duties. The South Brunswick Police Department was the first agency in New Jersey to acquire an in-car computer mobile data terminal system, a policing tool Kane is now thoroughly familiar with.

The 71 auxiliary state troopers with the Vermont State Police, one of eight state police/highway patrol agencies that utilize reserve troopers, work extensively in marine enforcement and worked 13,000 hours last year in that area alone. In addition to their state police academy stint, they even get two days of training with the U.S. Coast Guard on marine issues.

Service in reserve law enforcement provides administrators a viable pool of talent from which to draw. The lower cost of identifying those who may be "badge and gun happy" is facilitated by closely supervising volunteer or part-time personnel. On the other side of the desk, the young officers themselves are afforded an opportunity to assess the viability of police work as a career choice.

Dr. Richard Weinblatt

April 1993
Law and Order:
The Magazine for Police Management

Reserve Detectives

In Tampa, FL, Auxiliary Police Officer Bill Schimmenti's wife has gotten used to having the ubiquitous beeper around. When it goes off, it's the Tampa Police Department requesting Schimmenti's presence at yet another homicide scene.

Schimmenti is one of many reserve police officers across the United States who serves as detectives. While most volunteer or part-time reserves, known in some jurisdictions as auxiliary or special officers, discharge their service in uniformed patrol, a growing number of agencies are successfully utilizing reserves as investigative personnel or in similar roles. Among the departments, large and small, that utilizes reserves as detectives are: Cass County Sheriff's Office in Fargo, ND; Douglas County Sheriff's Office in Omaha, NE;

Harris County Sheriff's Office in Houston, TX; the Honolulu Police Department; and the Seattle Police Department.

The suburban Los Angeles Orange County Sheriff's Office (based in Santa Ana) has 15 reserve investigators. Also in California, the San Bernardino County Sheriff's Office, with more reserves officers than full-timers (1,091 reserves, 980 salaried), uses reserves in arson and narcotics investigations.

Reserve investigator functions run the gamut from plainclothes buy and bust operations involving part-time deputy sheriffs of the Rockland County Sheriff's Office, in the shadow of New York City, to the undercover narcs of the Houston-based Harris County Sheriff's Office. Yet another example is the background investigations and interviews conducted in part by senior South Brunswick Township, NJ, auxiliary officers for auxiliary police officer candidates.

In Memphis, TN, the Shelby County Sheriff's Office director of reserves, B.J. Patterson, said his 280 reserve deputies, like the 800 full-timers, are screened and get 430 hours of basic training. "We use reserves in all areas including solo patrol, patrol as a second deputy, motorcycle, interstate drug interdiction patrol, warrants and narcotic investigation."

Dr. Jim Kimmelman, a periodontist armed with a D.D.S. degree and Shelby County detective bureau business cards, uses his training as a biologist to conduct investigations at crime scenes. "I reached a point in my life where I felt that I owed the community something," related the doctor who graduated from the academy in 1986 and joined the detective bureau four years ago after initially serving in crime prevention. He now commands 25 reserves who, in the trendiest detective style, wear ties and carry firearms and six-point star badges on their belts.

Crime scene car #340, a 1991 Chevrolet Caprice sedan is manned every night of the week by volunteer detectives. "The car is fully equipped to handle burglaries, suicides, kidnappings, and homicides. We've already had most major types of crime scenes under our belt," Kimmelman said proudly. His detectives also work with other agencies including the Memphis Police Department and the FBI.

Robert W. Ladley, who owns a locksmith business, graduated from the police academy with Kimmelman and works as his partner. He recalled that their first case was a homicide. "A local man was shot in the head and we worked the whole case. The man's six-year-old son, along with the physical evidence gathered at the scene, was important in resolving the case." He added that such gruesome assignments have led to Kimmelman the dentist being nick-named "Dr. Death."

Tampa's 800-officer police department has an additional 25 reserves and 55 auxiliaries with three volunteer law men assigned to the detective division. Two are reserves and one is a homicide auxiliary detective. Under Florida statutes, the Sunshine State's 2,659 reserves have the same 520 hours of training and authority as the 32,212 regular officers. The 2,674 auxiliaries, with at least 97 hours of training, have authority only while on duty and supervised. The city, like many jurisdictions, exceeds Florida Division of Criminal Justice Standards and Training regulations by requiring 570 hours for full-time and reserve officers and 132 hours of basic training for auxiliary officers.

Tampa's Auxiliary Detective Schimmenti handles weekend homicide calls and always has his beeper nearby. "Sometimes I'll get a ride with my full-time detective partner, or I'll go straight to the crime scene," he said. His attire ranges from tie, jacket, badge and gun to jumpsuit and firefighter boots ("for messy crime scenes"). Stakeouts sometimes require a more creative fashion flare.

Schimmenti, who used to work in the medical examiner's office, added that if it's a slow murder weekend, he'll put on a uniform and riude in a marked unit with a full-time officer. The 14-year veteran auxiliary officer has served the last six assigned to the detective division.

The volunteer detective's part-time status assisting his full-time counterparts on weekends necessitates some investive solutions to problems. "I can't have witnesses call me at work, so I use my partner's office number. He picks up the slack for me during 9-5 hours," Schimmenti said.

The Seattle, Los Angeles, and High Point, NC, police departments use their reserves in a different capacity as detective follow-ups. Major Wayne C. Hartley, who oversees the detective bureau of the 180-strong High Point Police Department, views the utilization of reserve detectives as good community relations. Cases with a lower solvability factor are given a higher amount of police attention than would be normally possible due to the understaffed regular detective corps.

"We use reserves on cases that might not normally be assigned out," Hartley said. "The public appreciates the attention and the reserves do sometimes come up with solid cases."

North Carolina's 8,037 full-timers and 2,009 reserves on the police level receive the same 432-hour North Carolna Criminal Justice Standards Division-mandated training. The state has a total of 16,526 regulars and 4,617 reserves, some of whom have to meet a different standard, such as the 4,818 full-time and 2,608 reserve deputy sheriffs who are trained a minimum of 444 hours.

High Point's top volunteer cop, R.J. Culler, said that the equal training makes it realistic to use some of his 18 officers as detectives when needed. In an era with an increased emphasis on community relations, High Point's program, like Seattle and Los Angeles, goes a long way towards assuring the public that the police do care.

Seattle's Lieutenant David Malinowski, commander of the special activities section which oversees his department's 50 260-hour trained reservists, said their reserve officers work with detective units on follow-ups. In Los Angeles, some of that agency's 650 reserves don suits and work as one-man, unmarked units on cold cases such as residential burglaries. Supporters of the creative deployment of reservists point to the fact that most break-ins are discovered in the evenings when people come home from work- the very time those reserves are most able to serve.

Proper selection of personnel to take on investigator duties is critical. Shelby County's Kimmelman said a healthy amount of uniformed experience is expected before a reserve could transfer. Seattle reserve police officers must have specialized assignments approved by the special activities section. Two of their reserves even serve 150 hours a month in the gang unit.

In Harris County, L. Ray Vickers, the chief of reserves, said candidates for detective positions must have at least two years' experience in the sheriff's department and pass an oral board. Harris County is "hard core" and utilizes many of their 316 reserve deputies in a variety of investigator slots including the Organized Crime Group (OCG) and pharmacological fraud investigation. One volunteer detective gained such a top flight reputation for building successful cases against doctors and pharmacists, the U.S. Drug Enforcement Administration hired him full-time to work at the federal level. Vickers contended that the undercover assignments made sense "since the reserve comes in as an unknown."

Specialized training, on top of rigorous basic entry and police academy hurdles, are essential to maintaining the professional integrity of a reserve detective program. Most agencies have some related training available to their reserve investigators and many reserves go beyond that level and acquire further training at their own expense. Many a reserve traffic fatality investigator has found himself in Jacksonville, FL, at courses taught by the Institute of Police Technology and Management (IPTM) or at Northwestern University's Traffic Institute in Evanston, IL.

In Shelby County, 40 hours of annual in-service training is mandated and is geared to the volunteer deputy's particular assignment. Kimmelman said that among the topics covered for his people have been latent fingerprints, crime scene photography and homicide investigation. The LAPD requires reserve investigators to go back to the famed Los Angeles Police Academy for a three-day course.

Hartley, harkening back to his own successful application of the reserve detective concept in the High Point Police Department, concluded: "To successfully do this, a reserve officer must have the proper training, some experience, and time available to do the job."

June 1993
Law and Order:
The Magazine for Police Management

Reserve Motorcycles: A Positive Public Relations Impact

The course was tough for the Prince William County, VA, reserve deputy sheriff. But the volunteer law enforcer completed the challenging, one week school at Old Dominion Speedway in Manassas, VA, which included braking on wet grass and negotiating cone patterns.

The course wasn't just your run of the mill police vehicle pursuit course, and the attendee wasn't just another officer. After earning the certificate, reserve deputy Nancy Tully became the first female certified in the Northern Virginia Criminal Justice Academy's motorcycle operations course.

With each component recognized for their public relations value and flexibility in deployment, it seems natural that reserves and motorcycles have joined together to serve their agencies and the public. Sometimes called auxiliaries or specials, volunteer and part-time officers in agencies large and small have found themselves increasingly riding atop iron steads as reserve policing permeates all areas of law enforcement.

Nancy Tully now rides as a team with her husband, Jim, a three year veteran who serves Sheriff Wilson C. Garrison, Jr. as a reserve corporal. They both donate 40 hours a month on their Harley-Davidson FLHTP bikes and Jim Tully was named reserve of the year by his agency.

The public relations benefits were cited numerous times by departments with reserve motorcycle officers. "Kids relate to motorcycles," Ridgewood, NJ, special police officer Louis A. DiGeronimo said. Often greeted with cries of "It's CHiPs," DiGeronimo said both children and adults in the 20,000 population Bergen County community are drawn by the magnetic presence that only a police motorcycle can create.

DiGeronimo and his charismatic leather clad comrades have found that the positive public relations impact they create upon arrival has become well-known throughout the New York City metropolitan region. Through mutual aid agreements and inter jurisdictional cooperation, the volunteer specials have responded to Union City, NJ, two years in a row for National Night Out and three years running for Mahwah, NJ's, March of Dimes Walkathon. Among the other agencies they've worked with are the Port Authority of New York and New Jersey Police.

Jim Tully and Nancy rode in the Presidential inaugural parade in Washington, DC, with the Federal Protective Service's motorcycle squad. The Prince William County motorcycle duo also works parades and funeral escorts, in addition to patrol.

The Los Angeles County, CA, Sheriff's Office has 963 reserve deputies and 20 of them assume the leather and steel persona. Deputy Sheriff Harry Porter, the full-timer who serves as the coordinator of the Sheriff's volunteer biker bunch, said his reserves work a host of assignments such as traffic enforcement, special events, departmental funeral escorts, parades and dignitary protection. Porter said they work out of his East L.A. office, but requests come in from various sheriff's stations.

"We do some DUI task force and seat belt task force, as well as some radar," added Wayne Low, the reserve captain who serves as the Sheriff's volunteer motorcycle unit's top cop. The 23-year department veteran, who has served for 21 of those years on an iron stead, said that among the more interesting events they work is the Rose Parade and the Academy Awards. They donate an average of 7,000 hours per year.

Because the 20 reserves are California Peace Officer Standards and Training (POST) certified Level I. reserves, with 391 hours of academy training (they exceed the state POST minimum of 214 hours of training for Level I. reserves) who may perform general law enforcement duties solo on duty, Porter said they had flexibility as to how to utilize the group.

In Memphis, TN, Shelby County Sheriff's reserve deputy Bob Hawks, the lone motorcycle reservist among the county's 280 430-hour fully trained volunteer officers, issues some 30 tickets a month. He also works escorts and school crossings. The agency has several reserve motors out of service, but should be back up to four soon.

Some departments do not have a cadre of reserves soley dedicated to motorcycle duty, but rather have a lot of qualified and approved volunteer motor officers from which to draw on when necessary. John D. Webster, the reserve captain and commander of the 20 commissioned reserves of the Middletown, OH, Police Department, said they pull officers from other assignments when motorcycles are needed. Webster, whose reserves are 450 hour Ohio Peace Officer Training Academy fully certified, explained that four officers have Ohio motorcycle endorsements and they draw from the three police motors in the pool of the department.

In Barrington, IL, volunteer officers used the department's old Harley for years. After the old cycle was retired, they equipped a member's Honda Gold Wing with decals, red and blue front lights and an extension light and now lead the community's parades.

While departments such as Middletown and Shelby County may have motorcycles on hand, for many the price of admission into this elite two wheeled club is steep. A look at the costs personally incurred for this specialized branch of reserve law enforcement, in addition to the motorcycles, often includes uniforms and training. After paying for his own firearm, Jim Tully shelled out $10,000 for his motorcycle. The Sheriff provided the uniform, radio and other equipment.

DiGeronimo said he paid $10,000 for his 1986 Harley Davidson FLHTP. The 51-year-old architect who also owns a restored 1968 Harley Davidson FLHP, which he used to use for police work, said the Ridgewood unit has five Harley Davidson FXRP or FLHTP models, as well as two Kawasaki 1000s and one Honda 1200cc. "A new guy will be coming on board and he just bought a 1993 Harley Davidson FLHTP for $13,000."

Ridgewood supplies the radios and equipment. The officers are attired in agency provided uniforms which are made up of an eye-catching collaboration of a three-quarter length leather jacket, leather strap, French blue shirt, yellow striped navy blue pants and leather boots.

Porter estimated that minimal initial expenditures for boots and breeches in L.A. County run the reserve deputy around $500. He said a new Kawasaki costs around $7,000, while a used one is $2,500. After the initial expenditures, the county picks up the tab.

With such large amounts of monies involved, insurance and other related matters are addressed via several different avenues. Los Angeles County reserve motorcycle deputies lease their privately purchased bikes to the county for $1.00 a year. This is a legal device to provide insurance, maintenance and gas. "The department supports us now," Low said in pointing out that no major injuries have occurred in recent years. "In the early days, the only thing the department gave us were "E" ("exempt" government) license plates."

Tully and his wife, Nancy, both full-time IBM employees, carry their own insurance. Ridgewood's officers carry their own insurance and the municipality has blanket insurance which insures them from the time they leave home on official business.

Low, who spent a year and a half as a Los Angeles Police reservist before joining the county, said the motorcycles are taken home but that their use is strictly governed; pleasure cruises are prohibited. Unusual circumstances must have departmental approval. "The reservist can only ride in uniform, even if it's going to the dealer for maintenance."

Ridgewood officers, who also take their cycles home, are issued cold weather gear and ride 12 months a year. Jim Tully, the first reserve cyclist had to purchase his motorcycle so he keeps it at home. Nancy has one courtesy of the department. It is stored at the agency, about a mile from their home.

Training, beyond basic law enforcement academies, is a concern for many agencies. In-service training agendas involving cone patterns and riding skills refreshers are present in all motorcycle programs. The Tully team went through the one week Northern Virginia Criminal Justice Academy basic motorcycle certification course which was paid for by the sheriff's office. IBM is high on volunteerism and gave them the time off to attend the course.

DiGeronimo said Ridgewood has approved plans for the special officers to go through the one week course put on at no cost by the Jersey City, NJ, Police Department. They had also considered the two-week New York City Police Department course, but it was too difficult for many of the volunteers to get that much time off.

Porter said an internal, individually tailored 80 hour training course is taken after the reserve deputy completes a six month probation period. Low said all reserves who want to transfer into motorcycles must have two years' experience at a patrol station and undergo a battery of challenges including oral interviews.

"They can't even buy a bike until they're off probation," Low said of those who are accepted into the elite unit. He explained that they are a self-sustaining unit with radio car support for prisoner transport, so reserve deputies on probation in the motorcycle unit work the cruiser.

All agreed that the costs, training and hurdles were worth it. "There is such camaraderie among motorcycle officers," Jim Tully exclaimed. "This is really exciting."

August 1993
Law and Order:
The Magazine for Police Management

Reserve Data Available: New Book Provides
Everything You'll Want to Know

A reserve police unit (also called auxiliary, special, etc. depending on local laws and regulations) is the ultimate in community policing. Such a force puts the police in the community and the community in the police, bridging the gap between cop and citizen.

Reserve policing may also be a recruitment stepping stone and testing ground of sorts for young adults contemplating a career in law enforcement.

However, some non-believers claim that this column highlights only the very few departments that utilize the sophisticated, highly screened, trained and deployed version of reserve law enforcement. The continuous stream of material published, not just in this column, over the past few years should have convinced everyone except the most cynical that solid programs are the rule and not the exception.

It is only fitting that the issue, the second anniversary of this column, announces the availability of a book which provides definitive evidence supporting our views on the topic. The book, *Reserve Law Enforcement in the United States*, is the result of a joint project of the Center for Reserve Law Enforcement, Inc. and the New Jersey Auxiliary Police Officers Association, Inc. (NJAPOA).

The 250 page book features countless facts culled straight from the source agencies and states and was a year in the making. As the author of the book, I intended for the volume to serve as a reference for anyone needing information on reserves. The book's foreword is written by James C. Lombardi, the reserve officer in charge of the Los Angeles Police Reserve Corps. and president of the California Reserve Peace Officers Association.

The Center for Reserve Law Enforcement and the NJAPOA went to whatever each respective state calls their regulatory agency overseeing law enforcement standards (Police Training Commission, Peace Officer Standards and Training Board, etc.). We learned from them how many full-time, part-time and volunteer officers were in their state and what their minimum training standards are for each category. In a reader-friendly format and alphabetized for easy reference, one to two pages profile each state's reserve-type of officers.

Graphs and charts utilize two main areas of data: numbers of officers in each category and comparisons of the training hours for those officers. At the bottom of the states' profile, a contact with address and phone number is noted if the reader needs further information.

In another section, the reserve programs of some 75 of the largest county and municipal law enforcement agencies are profiled. Again, contact names are given and the agencies are list alphabetically. Photos, charts and graphs, along with some department shoulder patches, break up the text.

The county and city section of the book reveals such agency specific tidbits of information as: how long the academy is and it is scheduled, who pays for the training, firearms, uniforms and equipment; whether the uniform is different from those worn by the salaried officers; how many hours the reserves served last year; and what duties they undertook during their police time; how long the field training officer (FTO) program is; and in-service training available to the non-full-timers. Also covered is the minimum age for officers and what kind of screening process they must undergo before pinning on a badge.

Another section of the book briefly covers reserves in other countries. It seemed unfair to dwell on the work done in the U.S. without acknowledging the similar sacrifices being made throughout the world. For example, England has 25,000 volunteer special constables, the Royal Hong Kong Police has 5,400 auxiliary officers, and even Bermuda has an 84 member volunteer officer contingent including an eight officer marine section.

The second section of *Reserve Law Enforcement in the United States* covers previous surveys that were done of reserve programs in years past including the well-known Arlington County study of 1969.

Before each of the two main courses of the book, there is a comparison of the individual profiles' data with others of its type. Suffice to say, the state regulations covering the training of a reserve in, say, Iowa differed from those applied to a reserve in Utah. Some of the percentage comparisons of full-time versus non-full-time were interesting. In Vermont, 65% of the officers are either volunteer or part-time paid. In Maine, the percentage of non-full-timers is 44, while in New Hampshire it's 43. Ohio has a little more than half, 55% of its officers as non-full-time officers.

Around half the states, including states such as Alaska and Michigan, do not have standards in place for all or some component of their non-full-time officer personnel. Surprisingly, one state told us they had no minimum standards in place for any officers- full-time, part-time or volunteer. They leave it to the local agency's discretion. Fortunately, in this litigation conscious world we work in, local law enforcement leaders mandated at least some form of training for their reserve officers. Even states where standards do exist, local jurisdictions and academies usually exceeded what is required.

Many departments have the exact same training hours and curriculum expected of full-timers for reservists. Only the time-frame in which to acquire the training is stretched out over evenings and weekends to accommodate the dictum.

The two last major sections in the book profile the eight state police/highway patrol agencies that use volunteer/part-time troopers and the large state reserve associations. As before, contact information is included in each profile.

The evidence this book provides is clear. This reference will be of invaluable assistance to anyone aiming to institute or revamp a reserve officer program. They will be able to pull out information on specific state and local practices, and the listed contacts make it easy to reach out for more information if needed.

This work is a testament to the laudatory manner in which volunteer and part-time officers are supporting the efforts of their full-time brethren in addressing the crime and quality of life concerns in our neighborhoods. The mountain of evidence contained therein is just the tip of the iceberg.

Dr. Richard Weinblatt

Summer 1993
21ˢᵗ Century Policing
New Jersey Police Community Relations Officers
Association

Volunteer Officers and Community Policing

In the spirit of police executives across New Jersey and the nation, Mount Holly Police Chief James F. Hansen explained how his 2.9 square mile Burlington County municipality was divided into eleven sectors with a police officer taking responsibility for two to three sectors in order to address quality of life concerns. The importance of joining the police and the community as a team to tackle problems has been clearly established.

What stands out about Chief Hansen's aggressive approach to the concept is that Class II. Special Law Enforcement Officer David Perez, a resident of Mount Holly, has responsibility for sectors also. "David is bilingual and it is beneficial for us to have such an officer who lives in a part of town where there are a lot of Spanish speaking people," said Hansen who added that Perez' duties also involve freeing up full-time officers for more pressing matters.

Hansen is not alone in the Garden State in utilizing auxiliary or special police officers to help bridge the gap between the police and community.

Considered to be the ultimate in community policing, this approach brings the community into the police and the police into the community.

Police officers tend to associate with other officers, whereas the reserve component of the department has ties to both the civilian and police segments. The auxiliary or special officer becomes the conduit through which each side gains an understanding of the positions of all involved.

Auxiliaries and specials have full-time jobs and assist their full-time counterparts on a part-time or volunteer basis. They receive their training and serve their agencies during hours which do not conflict with their full-time, day occupations.

In accordance with the Special Law Enforcement Officers (SLEO) Act of 1986, New Jersey special officers are certified by the Police Training Commission (PTC), the same body that regulates full-time officers. And they must complete their training prior to being deployed in the field. Special officers may or may not be paid at the discretion of the employing entity and are certified by a PTC approved academy at one of two levels.

Class I. special officers receive an average of 78 hours of training. They enforce municipal ordinances, Title 39 motor vehicle laws, and non-indictable offenses. They are unarmed, but may carry handcuffs, side-handle batons, etc.

Class II. special officers have full police powers and are armed while on duty. They undergo an average of 452 hours of training. Many academies exceed the 452 hours. The Gloucester County Police Academy in Deptford, NJ, conducts a grueling 625 hour Class II. academy.

Auxiliary officers in the Garden State are under the regulations of the New Jersey State Police Office of Emergency Management and may not be paid. They must receive a minimum of 42 hours of pre-serve training, although many academies far exceed that number. Essex County's auxiliaries get 77 hours of training in Cedar Grove, NJ, and Middlesex County's Edison, NJ, based auxiliary academy comes in at 88. Their service must be oriented to training objectives and they cannot replace full-time officers.

Auxiliary officers have full police powers while on duty and may be armed at the discretion of the Chief of Police upon completion of a PTC firearms course. Essex County, Bloomfield, Essex Fells, Irvington, Maplewood, Roseland and South Orange have armed, volunteer auxiliaries. The Passaic County Police Academy in Wayne, NJ, runs an 80 hour firearms course for auxiliary officers.

In Perth Amboy, NJ, Detective William "Willie" Lopez, the auxiliary police liaison officer who oversees the 188-member department's community relations efforts has put his auxiliary officers on bicycles on the waterfront and other key areas of the 52,000 population Middlesex County city. The 15 year veteran, who spent two years as a Los Angeles Police officer in South Central L.A., said the 33 volunteer auxiliary officers are the ambassadors of the city and help to reverse the negative image the community has of the police.

"We deal with people on a human level and break the macho cop stereotype that people have of cops," said Alvin Gautier, an auxiliary sergeant with seven years of service.

Perth Amboy auxiliaries have a directed patrol plan which includes the railroad station and downtown areas. Detectives have used the special officer as an interpreter in investigations including a rape case.

Auxiliary and special officers are often put in the field to tackle a particular type or geographical area problem. In Camden County, Haledon Township Class I. specials have been instrumental in curtailing underage drinking.

In the City of Long Beach, NJ, Captain Patrick Caron, Director of Public Safety, has used Class II. special officers on the boardwalk and during large events such as parades. The specials, who get 415 hours of training over the course of nine months at the Monmouth County Police Academy, have done well. He plans to use volunteer officers in the downtown section of the city to assist with foot patrols.

In addition to their basic training, the volunteers/part-time officers often go at their own expense to in-service training courses. It is part of the movement among reservists themselves to upgrade and professionalize. In great part due to the litigious environment that police administrators operate in, the old civil defense mentality is falling by the wayside as the higher standard and level of expectation is being applied to the officers.

Among the auxiliaries who have become Monadnock PR-24 certified instructors are Cranford's Brian M. Lopez, Eatontown's Thomas Gross, Perth Amboy's Michael A. Chrone and Bloomfield auxiliary sergeant William Vloyanetes who is a Doppler radar operator and a certified firearms and PR-24 instructor.

New Jersey's auxiliary and special officers, like the quarter of a million reservists who serve across the nation, have become an integral part of the law enforcement landscape.

Dr. Richard Weinblatt

July 1993
Police: The Law Officer's Magazine

Credence & Credibility: Training, selection standards, and liability still top the list of concerns about reserve officers. Increased professionalism, however, has brought increased respect.

Captain Mark Neeley is part of a dynamic nationwide movement. As president of the Alabama Sheriffs Reserve Association, his goal is to ensure that training in his state becomes the backbone of an effective and responsible deployment of reserves.

"The days of a sheriff (or police chief) handing a good old boy a gun and a badge are over. Reserves are involved in a serious activity, which can have serious consequences if they are ill-trained or poorly screened," opined Neeley, who works full-time as a personnel director for a steel company. He added that, executed correctly, reserve employees accrue many positive benefits for their agencies and the citizens they serve.

Such sentiments are not just expressed by one solitary volunteer top cop. Neeley, along with many other advocates of reserve officer training, are molding the new breed of reservists- screened, trained, and ready to take on the challenges of 21st century policing.

Part-time volunteer or paid law enforcers play an integral role in American public safety. They are called reserves, auxiliaries, or specials; each jurisdiction claims it own preference. Derisively they have been known as "wannabes," "hobby cops," and "weekend warrior." In many jurisdictions, their stereotypical image has recently been amended by their adherence to the principles of professionalism, which guide their full-time counterparts.

Reserves are employed by agencies from state police/highway patrol (11 states have volunteer state troopers) to county sheriffs to municipal police. They have found a niche in positions such as fish and game rangers and state attorney generals' office investigators.

Accumulation of Talent

Countless numbers of specially trained reserves donate their hours serving on special teams such as SWAT, K-9, search and rescue, aviation, narcotics, warrant squads and detective units. Agencies have taken advantage of the lawyers, doctors, accountants and other highly credentialed experts in the community. Their talents have been applied in a reserve capacity as forensic scientists, police surgeons, legal counselors and police psychologists.

Clearly what separates the active and integrated units from those that are less utilized are the components of screening and training.

"Our reserve deputies have the same authority and must go through the same screening- psychological, NCIC and motor vehicle," explained Lance Saylor, Sheriff of Williamson County, Tenn.

Saylor, an FBI National Academy graduate with a master's degree in criminal justice, is supportive of a professional reserve officer program. His 30 reserves handle many of the same responsibilities of 123 full-time personnel "provided they make it through the screening process."

Neeley said Shelby County reserve deputies undergo the same 280 hours of training as full-time certified personnel in the state of Alabama. To be considered they must run the gauntlet of in-house panel interviews, driving and criminal history checks, academic records and background checks.

In Olympia, Wash., Cappy Gagnon oversees 25 reserve officers. Reserves there go through "essentially the same screenings as regular officers." The screening components include background investigations, psychological, polygraph and an oral board made of a mixture of full-time and reserve personnel. Last year, Olympia's program took 10 out of the 80 reserve hopefuls who applied.

Screen Test

In San Diego, the county sheriff's department also places an emphasis on screening. Reserve Lieutenant Randy Dick explains how it is efficient to thoroughly screen the personnel and only 12 percent of the trainees in the academy. "Why spend the money to train them if you lose them along the way. There is no shortcut on screening"

"Our individuals on the street, whether they are reserve or regular, are comparable," said Sheriff Saylor. He is mindful of the liability involved in utilizing poorly trained reserves. "We make sure that the reserve candidate fits the same criteria. It gives me peace of mind to know that they're as sound as a regular deputy."

It is impossible to totally screen out undesirable individuals. The best protection is the utilization of screening standards that mimic those employed in the screening of full-time personnel

Who Are These Folks?

Who wants to put on a gun and a badge and come to the aid of strangers? Most reserves fall into one of two categories.

Some reserve officers have settled into civilian vocations and look to reserve service as a way of giving back to the community. They often express the desire to have gone into policing early in their life and are now settled in another field with responsibilities, which make a career switch unrealistic.

Other reserves, who are in the early stages of their job search, view their service as a way of getting their foot in the door for a career. On the other side of the table, management gets a bird's eye view of how the novice officer operates under fire. This sometimes saves the department from hiring a person ill-suited for the job.

"We've had five reserves hired as full-time officers this year," said Gagnon reflecting on Olympia's experience with the reserve-to-regular cop process. "Over the last eight years, 27 reserves have made the transition."

Training and Standards

"Liability (of reserves) is a function of their training," said attorney Howard L. Ekerling. "The evidence shows that, if the reserve is well trained, there is no liability." Ekerling, who is one of 10 lawyers serving the as LAPD reservists, admitted lawyers would be the last people to pin on the badge if the liability risk was not, in fact, minimal. He is also the general counsel for the California Reserve Peace Officers Association.

The funding for training of new reserves, not surprisingly, often comes from the reserves themselves. This is particularly true in states such as Arizona, California and Florida where community colleges provide the setting for basic training. The cost for training can range from $100 in Massachusetts for a 96-

hour "reserve/intermittent" school up to $3,000 under Pennsylvania's 520-hour program.

Charging tuition for the reserve candidate has another benefit. It allows the chief or sheriff to see how badly the person "wants it" and thereby becomes an additional screening tool.

"Our 280-hour certified reserves (in Alabama) can go right over to full-time if they want to," Neeley says. Most candidates complete the rigorous training in the evenings and on weekends, over the course of a year.

"No distinction is made between 280-hour certified full-time, part-time or volunteer officers," confirmed John Anderson, executive secretary of the Alabama Peace Officers Standards Commission.

Ekerling said Los Angeles' Designated Level I reserve officers "receive more training than the state requires for regular officers." (Officers in most departments exceed the minimum state requirements for training.) Reserves at that classification receive 570 hours of training at the Los Angeles Police Academy two nights a week and every other weekend.

Arizona, through the Arizona Law Enforcement Officer Advisory Council (ALEOAC), mandates that all officers, regardless of pay status, receive 440 hours of basic training. Ten ALEOAC-accredited academies are located throughout the state and are comprised of a combination of regional police academies and community colleges, making it more convenient for reserves to attend.

The same concept holds true in North Carolina. According to Scott Perry, deputy director of the North Carolina Criminal Justice Standards Division, all full-time, part-time and volunteer police personnel take 432 hours of pre-service basic training. In Wyoming, with four training locations, full-timers have one year to complete 403 hours of training while reserves have two years to acquire the same training.

Because of the positive orientation toward professionalism, many states have established identical training standards for full-time and reserve officers. Other states are moving in that direction. In a few circumstances, the reserve training may be used as part of the basic academy.

In New Hampshire, full-time officers receive 430 hours of training while part-time and volunteer officers undergo 100 hours of training. California, Colorado, and Idaho employ a multi-tiered level of training geared to the duties the reserve is slated to fill. In Colorado, for example, Class I reserves complete 358 hours of training, the same as full-timers. However, John R. Shell, director of the Colorado Peace Officer Standards and Training, explained there are three other levels of training. The lowest, 35 hours reflects diminished law enforcement duties and authority.

Where no minimum training standards have been set for reserve personnel by the state (such as Alaska and

Louisiana), some measure of liability protection can be gained from training under the auspices of an independent, third-party organization. Such a situation is preferable to in-house training, which is only a step above no training.

The Task at Hand

Once trained, reserves find themselves deployed in numerous ways. Some serve as "block watchers," functioning as the eyes and ears of police. More often the reserves are engaged in supporting the delivery of police services.

California reservists at all levels fulfill general law enforcement duties solo and have full police powers 24 hours a day throughout the state.

Sheriff Saylor said his Williamson County reserve deputies patrol with a regular or with a reserve supervisor. "One group of our reserves is training with the Special Emergency Response Team deputies," he said. Similarly, reserves in Olympia and Shelby County also patrol either with a full-timer or another reserve.

Applicable Appearance

In many states, it is impossible to visually distinguish the reserve from the regular. Slight differences in the uniform are discernible only to other law enforcement personnel. In Shelby County, Neeley said that their badges were silver as opposed to the gold stars sported by the full-time deputies. In Los Angeles, an "R" is put before the serial number on the badge.

Reserve officer safety, morale, and performance expectation standards are among the reasons cited for having little or no differentiation. Gagnon said that being identified as a reserve with the implication of being a second-class officer will lead the reserve to live down to the level of expectation.

In Marshalltown, Iowa, police reserve Capt. Daniel Brandt, said a demonstration in his area led to the removal of all distinctive markings. "They (the demonstrators) believed incorrectly that the reserves had limited authority and targeted them disproportionately.

"Differentiation is dangerous and ridiculous," said Gagnon, echoing the sentiments expressed by Brandt and others.

As law enforcement agencies strive for creative ways to meet budgetary constraints in the face of escalating demands of communities hit hard by crime, the role of professional reserve officers expands. Reserve officers, properly screened and trained, provide agencies a method by which they can supplement already strapped manpower allocations with minimal repercussions regarding negative liability or cost concerns. Administrators across the country have found their reserve and auxiliary programs to be a prime vehicle for observing the suitability of young men and women for full-time positions.

"We're just working to make sure that people are getting caught up to the times," said Shelby County's Captain Neeley of the increased emphasis on professionalism.

Dr. Richard Weinblatt

December 1993
Law and Order:
The Magazine for Police Management

Professionalism Reduces Liability: Trained Reserves Make Positive Contribution

A recent excessive use of force court case in Rhode Island resulted in a $650,000 judgment against a reserve police officer's employing agency. The officer had no training and the city was held responsible under the concept of vicarious liability.

"The vicarious liability for departments to put reserves out with inadequate training is quite large," David Ricciarelli, coordinator of testing and instruction at the Rhode Island Municipal Police Academy, commented.

Court cases involving reserves focus not on whether the officer is a reserve versus full-timer. Rather, the debate centers on the level of training the officer received to do the task he was asked by the agency to perform; the same question posed when a salaried officer is involved in a situation.

According to our survey recently published in the book *Reserve Law Enforcement in the United States*, half of the states in this country do not have state training minimums in place for all or some part of their volunteer or part-time officer contingents. In these cases, training decisions for reserves, who are also called auxiliaries or specials depending on local preferences, are left to local authorities.

Speaking from his Lincoln, RI, office, Ricciarelli said his state used to have a 40-hour state run training program but discontinued it a few years ago. "We did not have any state regulations, short of full certification, which defines what a reserve is and what training they should receive," he said. "We felt the state should not take on the liability."

The result was that many agencies in Rhode Island closed down their programs. Others ignored the state's premonition concerning the excessive use of force case and offered their reserves no training even on an in-house basis.

Among the many states that leave the use and training of reserves up to local authorities are Alaska, Louisiana, Michigan and Nevada. In the absence of a state's involvement of standards oversight, local authorities should settle on a bona fide training program if they wish to continue to utilize their reserves. Many good local programs abound with rigorous internal mechanisms to assure quality control.

Ideally departments would like to spread out training tasks and liability issues with the state. Given the premise that no such involvement is forthcoming, the next logical step is some other credible entity other then the employing agency.

In the southeastern corner of Michigan, Livonia-based Schoolcraft College offers local chiefs a creative training alternative which allows them to continue the use of reserves. Overseen by a body of 12 local police chiefs called the Reserve Advisory Committee, the 100 hour Police Reserve Officer Training program has held 32 graduations for over 2,000 reserves in its 15 year history.

The course is typically run on Monday and Wednesday evenings from 7:00 pm to 10:00 pm for 15 weeks including some Saturdays for range qualification. A firearms training simulator is used.

"Many departments require their reserves to graduate from our program," Douglas M. Purcell, coordinator of continuing education services for Schoolcraft College, explained. "Because this has become the standard for the area, their liability protection is better."

Purcell said the chiefs have direct input concerning the content via the advisory committee. The credibility and quality of training is enhanced due to the variety of expert guidance available.

Along the same vein, Lucien Pratt, chief of reserves for the Woonsocket, RI, Police Department, is aiming to put together a coalition of local agencies to form a regionally accepted basic police reserve training program. Pratt, the retired chief of the Rhode Island Park Police who has served as Woonsocket's reserve chief for two years, said his department currently utilizes a 60 hour in-house program which meets every Tuesday and Wednesday night at the local high school for 2 ½ months.

"We go over all of the important topics and of course thoroughly document all of the training dispensed," Pratt said. Among the topics covered are laws of arrest, car stops and report writing. His 55 volunteer officers help the 108 regular officer force provide service to the 40,000 population city.

Pratt lamented that he would love the state or an independent entity, a la Schoolcraft College, to conduct a training program. In order to maintain the professionalism and credibility they worked so hard to attain, banding together with others in the same predicament seems to be the next viable alternative for Pratt and his colleagues in Rhode Island.

"The New Jersey Auxiliary Police Officers Association (NJAPOA) is the only affordable, independent source of training we've found to send our officers to," Pratt said. Woonsocket reserve officers have driven all the way to the Garden State to take NJAPOA in-service courses such as traffic direction and motor vehicle stops. The organization of New Jersey auxiliary and special law enforcement officers offers a variety of courses for full-time, part-time and volunteer officers including PR-24 Instructor, Defensive Tactics and Community Relations.

Pratt predicted that the cooperative efforts of local agencies to create a training entity would go a long way to alleviate the training concerns.

As for in-house training, the smartest move is to mimic all of the requirements as set forth for the full-time officers. All of the states, with the exception of Hawaii, have state imposed minimum training standards for full-time officers.

The Louisiana Commission of Law Enforcement in Baton Rouge, LA, regulates only full-time officers who must have a minimum of 240 hours of basic training. While some agencies in the state do not formally train their reserve officers, the New Orleans Police Department puts their 175 reserve officers through a 500 hour police academy, just like the 1,300 full-time New Orleans officers.

The eight month academy takes place on Tuesday and Thursday evenings and all day Saturday for eight months. Reservists perform the same duties as regular officers and must donate a minimum of 24 hours of service per month. Even their field training officer (FTO) program is challenging and mirrors the full-time FTO process with a requirement of just over 300 hours.

Given the complex problems that may arise with the use of reserves in an urban environment, the administrators of New Orleans' well-structured program have protected (legally and otherwise) the city and its citizens by ensuring that reserves meet the identical entrance, training and deployment standards as set for salaried officers.

Nevada is in much the same situation as Louisiana. Nevada's Peace Officer Standards and Training organization, based in Carson City, NV, also regulates only the full-time component of law enforcement.

Like other reserves in Nevada, Reno's 70 police reserves need only meet standards set by their local employing agency. The 285 officer department has its full-timers trained to 600 hours, but allows reserves the option of either 600 hours or 480 hours. The 480 hour reserve academy is held on Saturdays, but only 25 of the 70 reserves chose the lesser route. All Reno officers, 480 hour reserves or 600 hour reserves and full-time officers, must also undergo a 560 hour field training officer (FTO) program.

Among the states that do have standards for reserves, the most popular method used is a modular or level system. The local chief or sheriff is able to select the extent of involvement he would like to see his reserves operate under. Different levels of training, approved and certified by the state, are available with a job task and comparable training philosophy in mind.

This method is extremely popular with propoenents of reserve training and has met with much success in California, Colorado and Idaho. For example, Idaho reserves, all of whom are armed, may be deployed for duties compatible to one of three levels of training. According to the Idaho Peace Officer Standards and Training Academy in Boise, ID, Level I. reserves are fully certified by the state upon completion of a 160 hour academy. They must also take 120 hours of in-service training annually.

Another option for Idaho is Level II. reserves with at least 25 hours of state mandated training, non-certified with regard to police powers and must work under the supervision of a full-time officer. Level III. reserves have no state imposed minimum training and are used only in specialized functions such as mounted posse and parades.

In Illinois, the training standards for volunteer and part-time officers have been an issue of hot debate for several years. The Illinois Local Governmental Law Enforcement Training Board does not currently require Illinois' 2,738 part-time and 2,085 volunteer officers to take any training except for a 40 hour firearms course if they are armed. Training is left open to the local chief or sheriff.

However, change is coming. The Chicago metropolitan area arm of the state training board has developed a four tier model program, to be taught in the evenings and on weekends, based in part on California's approach to the problem.

Phil Brankin, director of Northeast Multi-Regional Training Mobile Team Unit Three, the entity spearheading the Illinois modular training experiment, said, "Our job is to train police officers whether they're full-time or part-time." His outfit has been offering an extensive menu of in-service training to both regular officers and non-full-timers in the region. But the training of part-time officers has been neglected at the state level.

The program, broken up into four modules, has been approved in concept, but the specific components of the training need to be approved by an oversight body. Brankin, a former police lieutenant who has held the directorship for two years, predicted that things should start rolling after the first of the year.

"A chief can use as many modules as he feels the reserve officer's duties dictate. It will be his call what extent of training his officers take," Brankin explained. The sections are based in part on a job task analysis done in 1982 by the training board in Springfield, IL. "Local chiefs have been very supportive. They've helped us identify what blocks of training should be in each of the modules."

Brankin's goal is to have each of the approved modules, which add up to the full-time officer 400 hour state imposed minimum training standard, combined for those who complete them. The purpose is to make the officer eligible to sit for the Illinois police certification test.

Brankin's concept appeals to the likes of Woonsocket's Pratt. What surprises many is that it is the reserves of Woonsocket, RI, as well as Reno, NV, and elsewhere, who are the proponents of solid police training.

On the other side of the desk, chiefs and trainers are also on a quest to make sure that all officers, regardless of type, are trained to the fullest extent possible. Being creative and seeking alternative means to provide that training is essential if reserves are to continue their ascent up the ladder of professionalism.

Dr. Richard Weinblatt

June 1994
Law and Order:
The Magazine for Police Management

Seasonal Reserves: Part-time Paid Personnel Fill in the Gaps

The majority of the reserve officer programs we've detailed in this column have been volunteer in nature, however, some are comprised of compensated part-time officers who serve on a seasonal basis. Many law enforcement agencies find their resources overwhelmed during seasonal or special event periods.

Such peak periods of demands for police services require a more intensive interval of full-time commitment than many volunteer reserve, auxiliary or special officers may be able to provide given their occupational and family responsibilities. In those cases where it is unfeasible to fill the gap with volunteer officers, many administrators have turned to part-time paid personnel.

Daytona Beach, FL, is one of the most recognizable names in seasonal law enforcement due to their identification with spring break. The 213 full-time officer city police department has up to 100 part-time officer slots which enable them to expand their ranks during the heavy January through April period.

These fully certified part-time officers pay their own way through local community college academy settings to earn their 520 hour minimum Florida Division of Criminal Justice Standards and Training certification. They are recruited in September as they graduate from the course and put through a thorough background check.

Officers accepted start policing the last week in January. "Speed Week," the eventful two week period which begins with the Rolex 24 Hours of Daytona and concludes with the Daytona 500, attracts an extra half a million people to the normal population of 64,000. Among many other events the busy season brings is the onslaught of the MTV-generation during the four weeks of Spring Break with its 300,000 attendees.

"We use these part-timers just like full-time officers. Nothing indicates their status, and we use them on bike patrol, on foot and in zone cars," Al Tolley, the public information officer for the Daytona Beach Police Department, said. Only the badge serial number differs from the regular officers. He added that the agency does not alter full-time staffing levels due to the use of the fully certified part-timers. They are used as an addition.

Tolley said the part-time officers work on an almost full-time basis during the bust four month period. With pay pegged at about $7 an hour, the heavy schedule enables them to "earn up to what a full-time officer makes minus benefits."

Also caught in the spring break syndrome are the agency responsible for policing the areas in and around Padre Island and neighboring Mustang Island in Texas. With a much smaller salaried payroll than an agency the likes of Daytona Beach, these departments find the use of part-time, paid seasonal help, along with volunteer reserve officers, to be a particularly indispensible part of their organizations.

Located on the northern tip of Mustang Island, the Port Aransas Police Department, with its ten full-time officers, five dispatchers and five volunteer reserves, makes good use of their four part-timers who are the officer primarily detailed to tackle the seven miles of beachfront open to cars and foot traffic alike.

"With the traffic and beach parking problems, everybody likes having them (part-time officers) there," Lieutenant Royce Iverson, a nine-year veteran with Port Aransas Police, said. He said the town population is normally 2,000 and as many as 100,000 jam the beaches for the 4th of July. "During spring break, cars are three and four deep on the beach."

Port Aransas also requires their part-time officers, who work Memorial Day to Labor Day, to be fully certified to state standards prior to applying for an opening. They may have gotten their certification through an academy as a volunteer reserve officer or part-time paid officer for another agency, or they may have paid their own way through a local course. The Texas Commission on Law Enforcement Standards and Education (TCLEOSE) mandates that all certified officers have at least 400 hours of approved academy training.

"The part-time officers take the load off of the full-time officers in town," Iverson said of his personnel who are armed and uniformed identical to full-timers. He said that they want the officers to be fully certified so that they are able to handle more than just parking and traffic problems on the beach.

Similarly, the elected constable for Nueces County Precinct 8, Ronnie H. Polston, said he has 10 full-time deputy constables and uses one part-time deputy constable who works from March through September. The agency also uses 50 volunteer reserve deputies.

Polston, who started his career as a volunteer reservist, said the part-timer assists with the six miles of Padre and Mustang Island beaches located within Precinct 8's 70 square land miles and 10 square water miles. The population of 100,000 people swells with an additional 80,000 people on the beach on weekends.

"We have thousands of cars with thousands of people on the beach," Polston, who is headquartered in Corpus Christi, said. He said that the certified part-time help is uniformed and armed like the salaried and volunteer reserve deputies and is issued the same pay check as a regular deputy constable except for the benefits. The difference is that the part-timer is not employed year-round.

Seasonal help certainly makes the difference for the Wildwood, NJ, Police Department. Considered one of the top three "summer special" programs in the Garden State (along with Ocean City and Seaside Heights), the city has only 42 full-timers to police a less than one square mile jurisdiction whose wintertime population of 5,000 explodes in the summer. With 52 liquor licenses, the potent mix of 100,000 young people from the Philadelphia region and elsewhere who pour into the close quarters Jersey shore community leads to an avalanche of calls for police services.

Captain Alan R. Aragon, a 24-year-veteran law enforcer who started out as a seasonal officer, said the department uses around 50 Class II. special law enforcement officers (SLEO) and is the state's largest employer of paid summer Class II. SLEOs. The department had as many as 80 prior to 1986 when stricter state guidelines went into effect.

Aragon said the deadline for accepting applications is January 31st. At the beginning of February, Chief Robert H. Davenport, also a former seasonal officer, and Aragon review the applications and schedule March interviews. Following psychologicals, successful candidates are sent in mid-May to the Cape May County Police Academy, located in Cape May

Courthouse, NJ, for an intensive, full-time, six-day-a-week academy for seven weeks. The almost 400 hour academy meets New Jersey Police Training Commission (PTC) performance objectives.

"Our special officers, who act as full police-powered officers while working for us, get out of the academy right before the July 4th weekend and spend eight weeks on the streets," Aragon said. The department provides the uniform and firearm.

"Wildwood is a transient town with people from New York City and Philadelphia," he added. "These officers are exposed as any other police officer."

Summertime isn't the only time seasonal paid officers hit the streets. In addition to marine enforcement and water rescue operations, which start in the middle of May, snowmobile patrol and enforcement in the heavy winter is the main assignment for the Vermont State Police's part-time paid auxiliary state troopers. One of only eight states in the country to utilize non-full-time trooper personnel in their state police/highway patrol operations (along with Alabama, Arizona, Connecticut, Florida, New Hampshire and Ohio), Vermont's 294 full-time troopers are augmented by a trained and armed contingent of 65 auxiliary state troopers.

According to Captain Thomas A. Powlovich, director of training and recruitment for the Vermont State Police, testing for the auxiliary trooper slots, which mirrors the full-timer selection process, begins in the fall of the preceding year. It takes six months to complete the battery of tests which include polygraph, physical, oral board, MMPI psychological and background investigation.

The auxiliary troopers are outfitted and equipped at State Police expense. The firearm is a Smith and Wesson 66-2 two and a half inch stainless steel .357 with a .38 load. The firearm is small due to their work on boats and other cramped area. The uniform, also provided by the agency, has an "auxiliary" rocker over the shoulder and the badge says "auxiliary state trooper."

Powlovich, a 17-year veteran of the State Police, said the auxiliary troopers are paid at the rate of $8.31 an hour and must be certified in accordance with Vermont Criminal Justice Academy Standards. Part-time personnel in Vermont attend a 50-hour core course, usually held over the course of one week, prior to beginning patrol work. The provisional, as they are called at that stage, then have up to one year to complete a 50-hour field training officer (FTO) program and 60 hours of elective subject law enforcement coursework which leads to their certification.

Wildwood, like the others, is inundated with applications sent by career-minded young people who look to their seasonal service as a stepping stone. The city receives 300 applications a year. "We've had summer specials go off into federal, state and local jobs. In Wildwood, 75% of the regulars started off as specials," Aragon said.

Daytona Beach's Tolley said the part-time officers enables the department to get a closer look at the officer and "let's the person see if it's the career for them." He said other agencies doing background checks on prospective full-time hires are impressed when told how the person successfully handled the enforcement pressures of spring break in Daytona Beach.

For administrators contemplating such a program, Wildwood's Aragon and the others stressed that training was the pivotal point upon which the success of the seasonal officer concept rests. "Training is the key," Aragon emphasized. "Incidents of police misconduct or things of that nature have subsided and there really is a relationship between increased training and decreased complaints against seasonal officers."

Dr. Richard Weinblatt

Dr. Richard Weinblatt

August 1994
Law and Order:
The Magazine for Police Management

Uniforms for Reserve Officers: Standards Vary Widely Among Agencies

Few issues regarding non-full-time law enforcement officers have become as heated as how to uniform reserve officers.

Some feel that the volunteer and part-time component (often called reserves, auxiliaries or specials) of policing should be distinctly attired, while others contend that differentiation is detrimental, and may even be hazardous. A few states mandate the placement of status identifiers on reservists' uniforms but the issue is mostly left in the hands of local agency executives, reserve administrators and sometimes even labor union representatives.

Rank Insignia

A big point in the debate of whether to identify officers as volunteer or part-time law enforcers is the question of rank insignia. Some volunteers, such as New York City's auxiliary officers, have a long standing rank structure which parallels the full-timers. Rank structure, and the accompanying heavy dousing of gold braid, is particularly prevalent among programs in the northeastern United States.

Many opponents contend that rank insignia leads to internal fighting and dissension, as well as civilian confusion as to who is in charge when situations develop in the field. In a Florida sheriff's department, a full-time deputy sheriff, who was riding with a clearly uniformed and rank-laden reserve lieutenant, incurred the ire of the citizen. When the man demanded to speak to the deputy's supervisor he was directed to the nearby reserve lieutenant. Not satisfied with the "supervisor's" response, the complaint was repeated to the department. Reserve ranks no longer exist in that agency.

Incidents have also occurred where civilians have ignored the full-time officer in order to speak with the reserve "sergeant." Such situations strain relations between regulars and reserves.

Tampa Police officials have minimized public confusion be eliminating the shite supervisor shirt that was worn by higher ups in the reserve and auxiliary components of that agency. While a minor amount of gold insignia is approved, all reserve and auxiliary officers, regardless of rank, wear the patrol officer's blue colored shirt.

Going a step further, the Seattle Police Department has a reserve chief, however his uniform is that of a patrol officer. Los Angeles also has a top reservist, but he too wears a patrol officer's uniform. The contention in these agencies is that the top reserve slots exist to help administer a vital public service program; not to become vehicles for egos.

Reserve organizations with ranks oftentimes become their own little world of political battles. The bottom-line mission of the reserve concept (public service) can get lost in a time-consuming maelstrom of jockeying for power and infighting.

Appearance Differentiation

Reflective of the trend to screen, train and deploy volunteer and part-time officers in a professional manner, distinctive markings, i.e. different colored uniforms or badges and patches which indicate status, are being toned down. Many agencies that used to have "reserve" on shoulder patches have dropped it. Some departments that had "reserve" printed on their badge have shortened it to an "R" indicator. There is no evidence any organizations are increasing the identifiers.

The Florida Highway Patrol is one of the few agencies that distinguish between certified and non-certified officers and the uniforms they wear. The difference is not based on the officer's receipt of a law enforcement paycheck; rather it is based on the level of training.

Not too long ago, the 12 fully state-certified reserve troopers (at least 520 hours of academy training and full police powers) had the word "reserve" removed from beneath their shoulder patches, as well as their badges and ID cards. The 589 auxiliary troopers, who receive lesser training at 97 hours, have "auxiliary" on their badge and patch and wear different colored pants (brown).

Survey

Information concerning uniforms was compiled from a survey of 71 agencies. The results were: 52% had their reserves wear an identical uniform to the full-timers, except for the badge, which was different in some way. 17% had them wear the identical uniform, including the badge, while another 17% placed their officers in the same uniform except for a different badge and shoulder patch.

Departments which had reservists at the extreme end of the spectrum with different uniforms, badges and shoulder patches came in at a paltry 11%. Only 3% had the same shoulder patch with a different breast badge and different uniform.

One example of the equal status, equal appearance concept utilized by 17% of those departments surveyed is the Shelby County Sheriff's Office based in Memphis, TN. Chief B.J. Patterson, director of reserves and emergency services, said their 280 reserve deputy sheriffs, who undergo 430 hours of training and have full police powers 24 hours a day, are identical right down to their ID cards.

In Houston, the 316 reserve deputies serving the Harris County Sheriff's Office are also indistinguishable from their full-time brethren. It's the same situation with the reserves of the Ada County, ID, and Cass County, ND, Sheriff's Offices. The Dade County Metropolitan Police in Miami have 50 state-certified reserves who look and are trained (700 academy hours) just like the full-timers.

With many of the agencies queried, different types degrees of separation existed even in those cases where distinctiveness is the mandate. As expected, different reasoning and motivations prompt the local edicts on the reserves' appearance. Most of the agencies stated that the difference, often only in the badge, existed for the internal identification purposes of the members of the agency.

The 67 reserve officers of the Dallas Police Department used to wear a distinctive "Dallas Police Reserve" patch, but it was replaced with the regular department patch for officer safety reasons. Said one reserve referring to their 768 hours of academy training: "We've earned the right to be treated as officers."

Same Uniform, Different Badge

Looking at a few of the 52% of the departments whose reserve officers or deputies have the same uniforms as full-timers but manifest their only difference in the badge, the distinctiveness of the "tin" is usually minimal. Again, usually only agency officers are able to pin down an officer's status.

"The public can't tell the difference," Rockland County, NY, Sheriff James Kralik said of his full-time and part-time deputies, both of whom are fully state certified. "There is no differentiation on the uniform. That subjects the deputy to danger and abuse."

Badges worn by Kralik's non-full-timers state "deputy sheriff" just like the salaried deputies. The only difference is that the 50 part-time deputies have six-pointed stars and the 250 full-time deputies wear seven-pointed stars.

In Marshalltown, IA, the police chief ordered the removal of reserve shoulder patches and other distinctive markings following a labor disturbance. Demonstrators identified reserves involved in the deployment and bunched up in front of them, bypassing the regular officers. "They thought the reserves would be more easily intimidated and more vulnerable," Marshalltown reserve captain Daniel Brandt recalled.

In a similar vein, the 100 reserve officers volunteering to serve the San Diego Police Department wear the same uniform, except for the badges, as the 1,990 full-time officers. Reservists sport silver badges, as opposed to the salaried officers' gold badges.

The Los Angeles County Sheriff's Office adds one extra digit to the serial number, but long ago did away with the designation "Reserve" on their 963 reserve deputies.

Sometimes volunteer officers are identified not on the basis of a law enforcement paycheck, but rather on the level of training received. Reflective of Florida's two-tier system, the Orange County Sheriff's Office in Orlando has their 80 fully certified reserve deputies (600 hours of academy training) identically appearing complete with five-pointed star badges. The 64 auxiliary deputies (160 hours of training) have a six-pointed star that says "auxiliary."

"R" For Reserve

Yet another variation of the many badge differentiation scheme by many agencies is the placement of the word "reserve" in small letters on the badge. Some cities, such as Middletown, OH, have "reserve" on the cap shield as well.

"If a citizen is close enough to read the tiny word 'reserve' on his badge, then that reserve officer has made a tactical error," Terry Lattin, a Seattle Police Department reserve officer and president of the Washington State Reserve Law Enforcement Association, said in illustrating the eye-squinting size of the letters.

A common marking on many of the nation's reserves is the placement of an "R" before the serial number. The

Los Angeles Police Department dropped the designation "reserve officer" some years back and replaced it with "police officer." The "R" before the serial number is the subtle tipoff discernible only to the insider's eye. The concept is followed by many other agencies including the Indianapolis Police Department.

In California, the Orange County Sheriff's Office imprints an "R" on the star and also the center state seal is unpainted. The 1,091 reserves of the San Bernardino County, CA, Sheriff's Office also have an "R" on their star, but additionally have serial numbers which indicate which level of state certified Peace Officer Standards and Training (POST) they have earned. The department's Level II. reserve deputies use 2,000 series badge numbers, while those at the higher Level I. training tier use the 1,000 series.

In Gretna, LA, reserve deputies with the Jefferson Parish Sheriff's Office have "reserve" on their badge and also have an "R" collar insignia to make them more identifiable to other officers. For the same reason, reserve officers with the Byram, TX, Police Department have a nondescript red band on their shoulder epaulets in addition to the word "reserve" on the badge.

Big Cities Differentiate More

Of the 11% of the agencies that place their volunteer officers in different uniforms with different badges and patches, almost all could be found in the largest metropolitan areas. Not surprisingly, the screening, training and corresponding duties of officers in these programs were at a much less sophisticated level than those who looked more the part elsewhere.

For example, Chicago's auxiliaries receive 16 hours of training, and are quite limited in their authorized duties. In Newark, NJ, the city police are in navy blue uniforms, while auxiliary officers receive minimal training, wear distinctive uniforms with light blue shirts, and drive vehicles with "auxiliary" markings on them. Interaction between the two departmental factions is minimal.

Adding a different shoulder patch to the appearance mixture were 17% of the agencies surveyed. In Virginia Beach, VA, the 60 auxiliary police officers, who undergo the same screening and training (520 academy hours) as full-time officers wear the same uniform with a badge and patch that indicates their volunteer status. According to Lieutenant J.W. Pritchard, the officers, who may carry their firearm off duty, "are exactly the same right down to state certification," with the exception of the badge and shoulder patch.

Higher Caliber of Reserves

Even in change-resistant areas hope is coming. The Washington, DC, Metropolitan Police has long outfitted their reserve officers in the same light blue shirt and patch that full-timers wear. The major change coming is that heretofore unarmed reserves will be receiving a higher, comparable level of training and be armed with Glock semi-automatic sidearms.

In an interesting twist, special officers with the Greenwich, CT, Police Department hit the streets uniformed according to the level of training they have obtained. All Greenwich specials, regardless of training level, wear a badge and shoulder patch that says "special." Fully-trained officers wear the same dark blue uniform as the salaried officers.

Special sergeant Eric Omdahl explained that the training is broken up into five one hundred hour blocks (for a total of 500 hours). After the first one hundred hour block, the non-certified officer is provisionally certified and armed and may patrol in a light blue shirt under the supervision of a certified officer.

While the phrase "clothes make up the man" (or woman) may or may not be true, the uniform and its accoutrements are a great indicator concerning the caliber of training and overall sophistication of a reserve program. The types of uniform often reflect the value and trust an agency places in its reserve officers.

Dr. Richard Weinblatt

Winter 1994
The Shield
New Jersey Auxiliary Police Officers Association:
N.J.'s Association for Auxiliary and Special Law
Enforcement Officers

James Bond Has Nothing on the Real 007: The Two Sides of Glen Rock Police Auxiliary Officer 007, aka Tim Hines

He could introduce himself as "Hines. Tim Hines." He wears Badge 007 and is Glen Rock, NJ's, real-life counterpart of Ian Fleming's master of weapons and defensive tactics- James Bond. Much like the character that has made the careers of Sean Connery and Roger Moore, Timothy J. Hines has had years of training, and that experience contributes to his ability to serve as an auxiliary officer for the Glen Rock, NJ, Police Department.

Hines holds a third degree black belt in Tae Kwon Doe and Hap Kido. He started his training trek many years ago under the tutelage of Master Byung Sun Cha of the USA Martial Arts College in Ridgewood, NJ. A volunteer officer for Glen Rock for two years, the 21-year-old martial arts expert says his training helps him to do the job.

"Martial arts training gives you discipline and confidence, "Hines said citing the reasons his parents enrolled him in the training when they divorced many years ago.

Even those with black belts have acknowledged the proficiency of New Jersey's own 007. Hines' list of accomplishments include winning first place in the state championship for fighting in the junior heavy weight black belt event in Ocean City, NJ, in 1987 and 1988.

Like many young martial arts enthusiasts, Hines had his share of street encounters in school. He said he went through the "tiger phase" when he was young and immature and needed to challenge the knowledge he was gaining. Later, he evolved into his current "dragon phase." He has "accepted the knowledge and doesn't need to use it unless absolutely necessary."

Convinced of the positive effects martial arts training has on young men and women, Hines shares his knowledge and teaches an average of twice a week at USA Martial Arts College. Many have encouraged him to open up his own school, but he says he wants to land a slot as a full-time officer, preferably in Glen Rock. "I want to be a full-time police officer and want Glen Rock since it is my hometown and is a very good department," said Hines. He worked for more than a year as a dispatcher in Midland Park, NJ, and recently started as a dispatcher for Glen Rock.

"I grew up in New York City in Jackson Heights, Queens. When I was little, a New York City police officer helped me when I fell off my bike. I work with young people now and hope to be involved in youth programs when I become a full-time officer," Hines said, detailing the roots for his interest in law enforcement. He currently serves as the advisor to the Demarest, NJ, Police Explorer post.

"I have noticed his efficient and good ability to get along with people," said Glen Rock Police Captain William T. Kealy, who has known Hines for five years. "He is professional, polite and gets along with the public and other police officers."

Kealy, a 19-year veteran and captain for two years, said he has noticed an influx of younger auxiliary officers interested in making a career in the field. "We had a couple of lean years, but in the last three years or so, we've gotten seven or eight new auxiliary officers who display a lot of enthusiasm."

Like James Bond, Hines doesn't rely on just one skill to get the complex job of a police officer. He is currently pursuing his associate's degree in criminal justice from Bergen Community College, and he recently completed a 134-hour emergency medical technician (EMT) course at the EMS Training Center in Paramus, NJ.

A volunteer firefighter in Glen Rock, Hines graduated from the Bergen County Fire Academy and he is also a graduate of the Bergen County Auxiliary Police Academy. Complimenting his extensive martial arts training is his status as a Monadnock PR-24 instructor. He attended the 32-hour course the last time the New Jersey Auxiliary Police Officers Association's NJAPOA Training Academy offered it.

"This is a terrific opportunity for the auxiliary officers," said Kealy, who holds a bachelor's degree in public safety administration. "They can see if law enforcement is what they think it is."

Hines and his ten fellow volunteer law enforcers help the 20 full-time officer agency (four civilians work in records and dispatch) to serve the 11,000 population, 2.5 square mile municipality.

The auxiliaries, under Auxiliary Chief John Greve, do a fantastic job for the borough. We've always been able to count on them," said Kealy.

"I think we have an excellent auxiliary program which has come a long way," said Hines. "I have learned a lot from the Glen Rock and Midland Park officers."

Glen Rock's local version of agent 007 has learned much in his 21 years. But like the sage and wise black belt holder he is, Hines knows that he has only hit the tip of the iceberg in his quest for knowledge. "I want to keep learning what I can in order to be the most professional officer possible."

December 1994
Law and Order:
The Magazine for Police Management

Liaison Officers: A Vital Link in a Reserve Operation

While it once may have been considered an appointment with no glory, or even an undesirable post, the slot of reserve liaison has gained stature and respect in many departments. Also referred to by the moniker "reserve coordinator," the full-time officers who oversee volunteer and part-time law enforcers are an integral component in determining the success or failure of a department's reserve officer initiative.

New Clout

Reflective of the strides reserve professionalism has taken over the last few years, liaisons too have garnered a level of clout heretofore not seen in policing. While they were once a dumping ground of sorts, Roger M. Moulton, the former Redondo Beach, CA, police chief reported that he had numerous applicants from within his agency for the liaison position. The resulting competition led to a formal selection process to make the appointment.

"A lot of departments used reserve unit liaison duty as a punishment and it was hard to keep officers in the position," said Sergeant Mark Bennett, a 16-year veteran of the Indianapolis, IN, Police Department who serves as the agency's full-time liaison. "This often reflected how the department perceived their reserves. In the past many merit (full-time) officers thought they were scabs."

Still other agencies use the liaison post as a temporary stopover prior to retirement. The result is an officer who has little motivation to push for his reserve subordinates and possibly rock the boat. Many officers in this highly frustrating situation expressed that few administrators would listen to them and that their program stagnated as a result.

Same Training

Bennett went on to explain that his 960 full-time officer agency uses their 62 reserve police officers for exactly the same duties as full-timers.

"They (reserves) used to be only wagon officers, but now they get the same exact training and do the same jobs in districts as merit officers," he said. He pointed out that both classifications of officer receive 500 hours of academy training and have to complete a field training officer (FTO) program.

The circle of proud reservists working for an equally proud liaison has been completed in Indianapolis. "The key is having someone who will stay in the position and will devote the energy and time," said James C. Lombardi, a much respected reserve top cop, echoing Bennett's sentiments. Lombardi is the reserve officer in charge of the Los Angeles Police Reserve Corps. and president of the California Reserve Peace Officers Association (CRPOA).

In California, long known for some of the best and most progressive reserve ideas, the Commission on Peace Officer Standards and Training (POST) has structured a 32-hour reserve coordinator course. For the last five years, a 16-hour update to the coordinator's course has been held at the CRPOA annual convention. Lombardi said the interest and the need is clearly present, as they see some 50 coordinators every year at the update course.

Key Ingredient

The installation of a full-time officer who understands reserves is a key ingredient in the recipe for success, Lombardi pointed out. Many a program has installed former reserves, who have since gone on to salaried status, to act as liaisons. This ensures a level of understanding not often present in those who have little or no exposure to reservists.

In Alabama, the Shelby County Sheriff's Department is an example of how a former reserve deputy, Chris Curry, became a regular captain with duties encompassing oversight of the reserves. Of course, few agencies have the political situation that led to Curry's appointment from reservist to captain, but the positive effect Curry is having is felt just the same.

Reserve Captain Mark Neeley said the communication between the 27 reserves and the Columbiana, AL, based department has never been better.

Similarly, in Atlanta, GA, Major Richard H. Davis, of the Fulton County Sheriff's Department, heads a rather large and sophisticated outfit which has gained national respect. Jumping over from his role as denizen of the car business in the private sector in Atlanta, Davis turned his volunteer commitment into a full-time position encompassing the reserves and more.

Stability, Accountability

While California's training for coordinators is well received, some opined that an exception to the rule is someone of the ilk of Indianapolis P.D.'s Bennett. "As a supervisor of full-time officers, there was no need to send me to specialized training," Bennett said. He embodies what reserve policing needs: supervisors who treat reserves as professional officers; not weekend warriors who have their performance assessed as a lesser level.

"We now have stability in the unit," Bennett said of his appointment to the role which assists him in accurate evaluations of the department's 62 volunteer officer personnel. He said that the reserve unit is authorized for 30% of merit (full-time) force strength (or 300 reservists) and that they were currently shooting for 150 reserve officers.

Implicit in the California message is the imperative that reserves be accountable and held to the same standards as those full-time, paid employees doing similar job tasks. While the majority of agencies do not have the screening and training resources the likes of those in Indianapolis, the charisma and leadership of a vibrant reserve liaison does not cost more than the malaise and averageness offered by a mediocre liaison.

The results generated by an effective reserve liaison or coordinator can be stunning.

Dr. Richard Weinblatt

February 1995
Law and Order:
The Magazine for Police Management

P.E.P. Program: Part-time Officer Training in Illinois

In December 1993, this column ("Professionalism Reduces Liability," L&O Vol. 41, No. 12) touched on a pilot program being proposed in Illinois which would give volunteer and part-time officers the ability to take 400 hours of training in a four tier program stretched over nine months of weekends and evenings. Good things come to those who wait, and for the dedicated non-full-timers who serve the communities of Illinois, the above proposal was no exception.

The Chicago metropolitan area arm of the state's Illinois Local Governmental Law Enforcement Officers Training Board, under the aegis of the Northeast Multi-Regional Training Mobile Team Unit Three's Phil

Brankin, the director, and Glen Huffman, the program manager, has made the plan into a reality.

Modeled after the successful tier or modular system implemented in California by a committee of local police executives, this Part-time Enhancement Program (P.E.P.) gives volunteer and part-time officers the training they need in order to meet their responsibilities. This type of training program had been discussed by the Training Unit for more than a decade but was never authorized by the state.

"While no one has yet stopped after completing a module, they can stop after reaching their duty level of responsibility. For example, an officer with only traffic direction duties could take only the first module," Huffman explained.

Huffman, a 26-year veteran of the Illinois State Police who left at the rank of captain and was police chief for three different Illinois municipalities over a nine-year span, is well respected for his part in spearheading the pioneering move towards accessible training. He reported that one P.E.P. site started their third module of training at the beginning of January and two other sites are gearing up for a February start. With around 40 in a class, 120 officers will be the first crop of P.E.P. graduates within a year.

Other sites outside the Chicago area are being explored and serious inquiries have been fielded from McHenry County to the west. "Area police chiefs have received this warmly," Huffman said.

Illinois does not require any training for its 4,823 total volunteer auxiliary or part-time officers, with the exception of a 40-hour firearms course. But most police chiefs recognize the liability involved in deploying poorly trained officers whether they be paid all of the time, part of the time or none of the time for their services.

David L. Blaydes, the class-elected president of P.E.P. class #94-2, said there is a misconception that part-time and volunteer officers serve in that role because they do not want to go through the hurdles required of a full-time officer. "Most are highly motivated individuals who are successful in the private sector and want to give back to the community or are interested in a law enforcement career. Until P.E.P., we didn't have a place to go for state-approved training.

Huffman said the 400-hour program meets Tuesday and Thursday nights from 7:00 pm to 10:00 pm and all day Saturday from 8:00 am to 5:00 pm for nine months. It's quite a commitment and one that the student officers are delighted to take on. "Look we're there for nine hours on Saturday on metal chairs," Blaydes said. "Most of these guys come to the evening class from work or leave afterwards to go to work."

Blaydes himself has his hands filled with the course, his family and a successful financial consulting business. On top of it all, Blaydes works many hours serving the 25,000 citizens of Villa Park, IL, as commander of the police department's 20 auxiliary officers. He has been an auxiliary in Villa Park for five years and served in Mendota, IL for seven years prior to that.

Six of the 20 Villa Park Police auxiliary officers are attending the P.E.P. program being held at the Glen Ellyn, IL, Police Department, even though Villa Park police chief Ron Ohlson already had his officers complete a 125 hour in-house training course which is not mandated by the state.

"I want all our officers, both full and auxiliaries, to have the best training available, so they can better serve their community," Ohlson said.

"The training copies hour for hour the basic course offered to full-time officers at the Police Training Institute," Blaydes said. He is understandably proud of the training he and his colleagues are finally receiving.

"Since our mission (at NEMRTU#3) is to provide in-service training, the P.E.P. enhances part-time and auxiliary officers who are already serving," Huffman said. He explained that participants in the program must be in an acting role as an auxiliary or part-time officer and they must be sponsored by their police department.

According to Huffman, all of the attendees have at least one year of street experience and a few have almost 20 years. An indicator of the caliber of officers taking advantage of the P.E.P. can be easily found as five have left already to take full-time positions. One went to the Cook County Sheriff's Office, and another went to the

U.S. Border Patrol and three others went to local agencies.

Among other requirements, attendees must pass three written exams per module. They also have to write two term papers during each module to ensure that they will be able to properly compose reports and the like. The setting is an academic academy. Stress is imposed by the student officers, working one, sometimes two, jobs in addition to the P.E.P.

Huffman said instructors are paid $35 per hour honorarium plus 25 cents per mile travel. Tuition for the P.E.P. doesn't exceed $3.50 per training hour and the total, including books and materials, comes to around $1,200. Some students pay all of their tuition, while others pay a part of it with their agency picking up the remainder of the tab. A few lucky ones have the fees paid for by their departments.

Huffman said he tells the P.E.P. participants that they are defining commitment with this undertaking, which involves a tremendous amount of personal time and sacrifice.

"We could be out playing golf or relaxing. We're here because we want to be," Blaydes said. He said there are plenty more like him who are just waiting for an opportunity to get the training that could keep them or a full-time officer alive.

Dr. Richard Weinblatt

April 1995
Law and Order:
The Magazine for Police Management

N. Carolina Reserves Among Top Ranked: Volunteers Find the Sweat and Hard Work Are Worth It

The career move that David Kale made in law enforcement is indicative of the respect reserve law enforcers have earned in North Carolina. Reversing the procedure of what many reserves do, Kale has served nine years as a volunteer police officer- following an 11-year full-time career in state and county law enforcement.

Currently serving as one of the Charlotte Police Department's top reserve officers, Reserve Major Kale discharges some of his countless hours of service high above the metropolitan area as an observer in a police helicopter. Kale and his 41 sworn fellow reservists, fully certified by the state, work mobile data terminal

(MDT)-equipped district cars solo, as well as a variety of other duties.

There are many opportunities for reserves," Jim Hoyng, chief of police for the 182 sworn full-time High Point Police Department commented. Hoyng's complement of reserve officers numbers 17. "Two of our reserves are trained hostage negotiators who have attended advanced training in Baltimore. One of them, Gart Evans, is an 11-year reserve who works full-time as dean of students for High Point University. He was a negotiator during a recent jail riot."

As with Charlotte, High Point's reserve officer are state certified having attended a minimum 432-hour basic training course at locations such as Guilford County Technical College or Davidson Community College. The time commitment is extensive. For example, Guilford County Technical College, based in Jamestown, NC, has a six month stint requiring attendance four nights a week and every other Saturday.

Chief Hoyng related how one young man, who has since joined the department as a salaried police officer, went through the 480-hour rookie school full-time five days a week for 12 weeks. That experience certainly cemented the perception that, as Chief Hoyng put it, "The reserves have been a great feeder system for the department's full-time officers."

In general, North Carolina's cities, such as Charlotte, Durham and High Point tend to run tight operations with clear policies and strict training mandates governing their reserve programs. Among the other agencies with respected programs are the Asheville, Greensboro and Winston-Salem Police Departments.

While there has been a steady trend away from the practice, anecdotal evidence suggests the county sheriff's departments still have a streak of politicism running through their reserve deputy sheriff operations. The indiscriminate handing out of badges and IDs has diminished, but is still alive and well in some North Carolina sheriff's departments.

As detailed in the book *Reserve Law Enforcement in the United States*, reserves in the Tar Heel state, serving a population of almost seven million people, stand out in a crowded national field of non-full-time law enforcement personnel. The state has set the tone for a progressive approach to reserve officer utilization.

With only one level of training for both reserves and full-timers, the distinction comes only in the form of municipal police officers versus county deputy sheriffs. Municipal officers must have at least 432 hours of academy-based basic law enforcement training (BLET), while deputy sheriffs get a minimum of 444 hours of basic training. The state has almost 5,000 reserves with some 3,000 reserves serving sheriff's departments and around 2,000 working for city police forces.

Several of those interviewed for this column cited only one main area that needs to be improved. The success that such states as California, Colorado, Iowa and Texas have had with the modular concept of reserve officer training is greatly missed in North Carolina where an aspiring reservists must take on the whole training challenge in one unbroken time frame.

"I don't know how these people do it," Chief Hoyng said. He is no slouch when it comes to hard work, as he holds three undergraduate degrees from Guilford College in Greensboro, NC, and is a graduate of the prestigious Southern Police Institute (SPI). "Our training course is a long hard process when you have a full-time job and a family.

But Hoyng's reserves, who serve the 46.7 square mile, 71,000 population municipality, aren't the only ones who don the uniform and sacrifice to serve their neighbors. In the city of Durham, NC, 50 reserve officers serve a minimum of 16 hours a month and are trained to the 500-hour mark, exceeding the state's minimum requirement. Durham's reserve officers, who carry an agency provided .45 sidearm, face a daunting academy experience three nights a week and some Saturdays for seven months.

But, as with full-timers, the training just begins when Academy commencement exercises are concluded. The heavily-documented field training officer (FTO) programs for reserve officers are hefty undertakings by themselves and come in at 192 hours for High Point, 480 hours for Durham and a whopping 960 hours for Charlotte.

The sweat and hard work appears to be worth it. Durham administrators stated that the reserves have saved the city a quarter of a million dollars a year. Kale, a bust and successful private sector businessman, said that Charlotte's reserves must put it at least 12 hours per month and that 14,811 hours were donated last year on patrol, as well as in such exotic assignments as the Street Drug Interdiction Unit.

High Point Police Department reservists work patrol, Tac Team, detectives, warrants and the traffic section, as well as being responsible for the coordination of special events such as walk-a-thons. Filling in some non-traditional gaps are the City of High Point's squad of specialized police reserves, such as lawyers and doctors, who bring rare and much needed skills to the agency.

High Point and Charlotte differ in one aspect. Chief Hoyng eschews the use of reserve ranks, citing the public's confusion and inconsistency with the department's philosophy of earned merit promotions.

High Point does use reserves to administer the program and do in fact bestow a good amount of behind the scenes responsibility starting with unit executive officer R.J. "Jerry" Culler. Charlotte uses a rank structure which is visible on the uniform.

Whatever the insignia, reserves in North Carolina have earned their place among the top-ranked reserves in the nation. They clearly have a solid foundation upon which to build for the future.

Dr. Richard Weinblatt

November 1995
Law and Order:
The Magazine for Police Management

Take-Home Cars for Reserves: Officer Effectiveness and Community Presence Enhanced by the Program

As the trend of utilizing take-home cars driven by full-time officers revs up in departments across the nation, so too are volunteer and part-time officers partaking in the advantages.

Referred to variously as reserve, auxiliary, special or supernumerary, this dedicated portion of the law enforcement community is no longer wholly relegated to the stepchild piece-of-tin member of the fleet car system which is being barely held together by baling wire and scotch tape.

The advantages of a take-home car- accessibility, long term cost savings, increased presence in the community and pride and care of "ownership" on the part of the officer- have also been put in gear for reservists. Expensive in the short term, the savings become apparent in the long run with the results being an extended period of service on the part of the cared-for take home unit.

Agencies large and small are putting off-duty officers in the driver's seat. Some are even allowing reservists to purchase their own units and equip them for duty, although the question of liability becomes somewhat murky when reserves take that path.

Sheriff Benjamin L. Montano, of the Santa Fe County, NM, Sheriff's Department, is among the progressive administrators who supports the concept. Montano said that when time is of the essence, reserve deputies who can respond at a moment's notice and proceed directly to an incident scene are vital to his voter-originated mandate of responsive law enforcement services.

The take-home car program has made a difference in Montano's agency, which provides police services to a 2,500 square mile jurisdiction with a 100,000 population. Prison escapes from the state prison facility, road blocks, and high risk search warrants are just three of the many examples cited by Montano.

"We can have roadblocks set up within seven minutes," said the 19-year law enforcement veteran, who formerly served with the Santa Fe Police Department. "Time is of the essence and the reserve deputies can respond immediately."

Short-notice extraditions to nearby locales such as El Paso, TX and Phoenix, AZ, can be easily handled by reservists and their units. Montano said that the reserves, vested with full authority to handle calls as a full-timer would, can go in-service quickly, often allowing a deputy to get time off in a personal emergency.

Santa Fe County's Captain Ron Madrid said the reserve take-home car program, in conjunction with the full-time deputy sheriffs taking their units home, lets them have "total police presence in the county." Enhanced community relations are yet another benefit, as the car is a visible symbol of law enforcement presence, helping it to seem almost omnipresent to the public.

Reserve Deputy Steve Branch, a four-year veteran who serves as a full-time firefighter in Los Alamos, NM, stated that he too thinks the concept works. "My neighbors come by, and it's good for law enforcement."

Madrid said the program, which currently involves five reserve deputies of the 15 total member reserve force, has never experienced a marked unit motor vehicle accident.

The Sheriff's Department reissues the fully marked cars to the fully deputized and armed volunteer deputies as they hit 60,000 to 100,000 miles of service under the steering of a full-time deputy.

All vehicles continue to be insured by the county. They are fully equipped with lightbars, sirens, radio, shotgun, etc. Radar units were even picked up from the New Mexico State Police in a cut-rate government deal for the rock bottom price of $20 each.

Reserve Lieutenant Tom Beaty, reserve commander, said that if the cars were sold at auction to the public, they would fetch from $500 to $2,000 each. Beaty said that some 4,200 hours were donated to the county by eight active reserve patrol deputies which amounted to a savings of $450 a month. He said the benefits clearly outweigh the costs.

The much larger Marion County, IN, Sheriff's Department, based in Indianapolis, also has an active take-home car policy for their reserve deputies (who receive approximately 600 hours of basic academy training at the Sheriff's Academy). The agency has 460 full-time deputies and 130 fully state-certified reservists.

Half of the reservists are provided with take-home cars. Those that are not assigned a car may borrow one from another deputy for the duration of the assignment. Take-home assignments are made on the basis of rank and seniority for the reserve deputies.

Deputy Chief Robert W. Leary, in charge of the Civil Division which oversees the reserve program, said they too reissue units after they have served a full-timer. For the past nine years, the take-home car program has seen the cars changing hands at 50,000 to 75,000 miles. As in Santa Fe County, the cars are fully equipped and are regularly inspected for cleanliness, etc.

Joe Brady, law enforcement sales manager for Diversifleet, Inc. of Kansas City, KS, which specializes in reselling used police cars, said that the 15-year-old company is a beneficiary of the take-home car trend. The company sells some 600 to 700 cars nationally and internationally each year.

"About 5% of our sales are individuals who are reserve officers," Brady said. He said that they take department trade-in cars, such as 1988 and 1989 Chevrolet Caprices and Ford Crown Victorias, and sell them to reserves for $2,800 to $4,000, depending on the mileage.

One reservist who bought his own unit is Ed Sanow, Reserve Corporal with the thinly-staffed Benton County, IN, Sheriff's Department. Sanow, who picked up his 1987 Dodge Diplomat from a local municipal agency in Indiana, said he uses the car as part of his duties as a member of the multi-jurisdictional Special Response Team. Sanow is the SRT's countersniper.

Sanow, a car enthusiast and the author of two books on police cars, said the vehicle is equipped with long weapons, full radio gear, and red lights on the front and rear decks, grill lights and wig wag headlights. He also has magnetic mount stars for the Dodge.

"The car lets me get to an incident scene very fast," said Sanow who paid $1,850 for the car which has 80,000 miles on it. He added that while gas, used on official business, is paid for by the government, insurance is paid by the individual and the liability also falls on him.

In Michigan, a volunteer police officer has a different twist on the insurance problem. Steven M. Kulakowsy, an auxiliary K-9 officer with the Flat Rock, MI, Police Department, has a contract with his agency which covers him, his dog and his equipped K-9 response vehicle. The contract puts the liability on the contacting agency.

Madrid said emphatically that he is happy with the response time of the reserves and their presence can be critical. "One of our reserves was even able to back up a full-time deputy who was involved in a shooting."

Santa Fe County Sheriff's Reserve Corporal Ted Chavez said he likes having the take-ome car because it enables him to serve the agency more efficiently. The former full-time officer recalled the time he nabbed a car-jacking suspect who fled Santa Fe's Villa Linda Mall.

"It would have taken half an hour to get units in place to stop him, and I was able to be right there and get him," said Chavez.

With such positive feedback from the deputies and the community, Sheriff Montano plans to expand the take-home car program for the reserves as his new batch of 15 cars for the full-time deputy sheriffs comes in.

"I have confidence in our reserves deputies and I don't know what I'd do without them. In fact, their badge says 'Deputy,' not 'Reserve.' Why not trust them with the car," Montano said. "The bottom line is: they can die in uniform like you or I."

Dr. Richard Weinblatt

March 1996
Law and Order:
The Magazine for Police Management

Reserves Patrol on Bicycles: This New Breed is Cutting a Wide Path as They Pedal Forth

Law enforcement officers patrolling on bicycles have become a familiar sight in many communities.

Not surprisingly, an ever-increasing number of those officers are non-full-time officers. Known in various jurisdictions as reserves, specials, auxiliaries, or supernumeraries, the new breed of bike officers is cutting a wide path as they pedal forth in communities from Iowa to Tennessee and California to New Jersey.

In Haledon Township, NJ, (population 4,866) six reserves officers have donned the police department's bike patrol uniform along with five full-timers. The department has a total of 17 salaried officers and 20 part-time paid New Jersey Police Training Commission-certified Class II. special law enforcement officers who carry department furnished semi-automatic firearms.

"I saw bike officers in New York State and offered the idea to our police chief," related Officer John Bachanes, coordinator of the Haledon Police bike patrol. "We are the first in Passaic County to do this."

Bachanes, a 15-year law enforcement veteran, said the bike patrol reinforces the community policing concept embraced by his agency as officers "get to know the community." The special officers magnify the effect given their unique status as they themselves are members of the community.

International Police Mountain Bike Association (IPMBA) president Allan Howard, a Dayton, OH, police officer, said that using bike patrols, particularly ones with reservists as a component, "falls in line with community-based policing." Howard's association comprises 1,600 members worldwide, with the majority in North America.

Many jurisdictions have discovered the benefits of using reserve bike officers. Jack E. Schlieper, chief of police in Mason City, IA, said that he has gotten good feedback from the community and likes the positive interaction between officers and the community. This has helped us address problems such as loud parties, kids in the downtown area and cars being broken into."

Schlieper said his reserves also pedal into mall parking areas and golf courses, as well as special events such as a recent Civil War reenactment.

Walnut Creek, CA, Police Department Reserve Sergeant Bruce Lesser, who oversees their bike program which uses only reservists, said that public relations is the big payoff for his upper-middle-class community located 15 miles east of Oakland, CA. "I probably engage five people in long conversations on the bike, whereas in a police car, I would encounter none." The 16-year reservist added that the bikes work well in his 15.1 square mile, 60,000 population city with 2,000 acres of open space, large retail district and extensive, unpaved trail system.

The Urbandale, IA, Police Department puts 10 of its 18 reserves on bike for at least 8 of their 16 minimum hours of monthly service. Reserve Officer Mike D. McFall said they started the reserve officer only bike patrol to "deter any problems before they started." In the upper-middle-class community which sits on the border of Des Moines, IA.

We have 15 miles of bike paths and parks which make this particularly appropriate," said McFall. He approached liaison Lt. Delbert King with the idea to start a reserve bike patrol in the 15-square-mile, 30,000 population city with a 36 full-time officer police agency.

It is mostly reserve officers that ride bikes in the tourist areas of Newport Beach, CA. Lt. Tim Newman, the

Traffic Services Commander who oversees the reserve bikers, said that the city's 70,000 population soars up to 100,000 due to the tourist business.

Six of the agency's 20 California Peace Officer Standards and Training (POST)-certified Level I. reserves are cross-trained on bikes. Level I. reserves in California are armed and are permitted to perform general law enforcement functions.

City officials in Newport Beach, CA, also think that reserve officers benefit from involvement in a bike patrol program. Newman said it is a fun detail which gives the reserves some variety.

Knoxville, TN, with its Old City section redeveloped with bars and shops, keeps its reserve bike officers busy in two-man teams, handling calls from 8:00 pm to 2:00 am on Friday and Saturday nights.

"The business community loves it," reported Lt. Doug Goin, the Central District Lieutenant and bicycle program coordinator. He said that the community relations aspects are beneficial and the two reserve teams on bikes answer calls for fights, disturbances, and the like. The agency uses eight of its 30 total reserves in the bike patrol.

The Mason City, IA, Police Department started their reserve officer bike program four years ago and it's still riding strong. "This is a good program as reserve officers feel independent and contribute more," said Cal Thomazin, a volunteer reserve officer and a district director for the Iowa State Reserve Law Officer's Association (ISRLOA).

Mason City's Chief Schlieper echoed Thomazin's sentiments. "We had to overcome the initial issue of supervision and we are now satisfied with the caliber of reserves we have and their use of radio contact," he said. The 45 full-time officer agency has a total of 20 armed reserves. The department's six reserve bicycle officers, who ride from April to October, are off the streets by 1:00 am.

Bikes and Uniforms

The IPMBA's Howard said that bikes "are a fiscally responsible alternative to increasing patrol costs." The trend to use bikes reflects the reality that police and sheriff's departments are like private corporations in that they are required to do more with less. "A foot patrol officer is restricted to four or five blocks, while an officer on a bike bridges the gap and covers more ground."

While the use of a reserve type of officer may not be a financial burden, agency administrators have to navigate the obstacles of the bike and the uniform.

Knoxville's Goin said that they arranged for the merchant's organization to contribute bikes. The department had an infusion of ten additional bikes purchased by the Housing Development Authority. The reserves wear the same attire donned by the full-time bike officers: a black golf shirt in the summertime and a black rugby shirt in the winter.

Chief Schlieper said the Mason City reserves bought their own white golf shirts, dark blue shorts and leather gun belt, which make up the bike officer uniform, saving the city this expense. He said that they are redesigning the uniform and will probably replace the leather belt with a lighter nylon gun belt. The city invested in two Trek 6000 bikes for the reserves.

The Walnut Creek, CA, Police Department also bought four Trek 7000 bikes, costing $700 each. The department's two original bikes, Whitneys, are used as backups. Reserve Sgt. Lesser said reserve bike officers obtain either nylon or leather gun belt and that the uniform consists of white shirt with black pants (short pants in summer and long pants in winter).

In Urbandale, IA, McFall said that their program is not costing the city anything. He stated that they used forfeited funds for the uniforms, which consist of a navy blue polo shirt and navy blue uniform pants which are cut off, as well as a leather duty belt.

Their two bikes were also acquired creatively. A $1,600 Pantera bike was confiscated from a drug dealer and a Roadmaster, which was found, abandoned, was forfeited to the city and put into the fledgling bike fleet.

Bike Patrol Training

Allan Howard of the IPMBA said that proper training is important for any officer, whether full-time, part-time, or volunteer, that serves as a bike patrol officer. His organization holds a 16-hour course which is approved by many states POST authorities.

Haledon Township's Bachanes said his five full-time officers and six part-time paid special officers went right to the bike pioneers. "The Seattle Police instructors travelled to New Jersey's Morris County Police Academy. We spent a week in the course where we learned how to use the bike in crowd control, how to draw your weapon on the bike and other important areas," he recalled.

Knoxville conducts a four day training program. The Newport Beach and Santa Monica Police Departments in California have their bike officers take a three day course. "They have to take three days off from their full-time jobs to take the bike course," said Santa Monica Police Lieutenant Phil L. Sanchez who serves as reserve coordinator.

Nestled on 9.2 square miles of land between Los Angeles and the Pacific Ocean, Santa Monica has 21 California POST-certified Level I. reserves with five of those bike certified. The 100,000 population city has 196 full-time officers with ten of those salaried officers assigned to the bike patrol.

Sanchez said the usual topics are covered in the training including strategic riding, tactical riding, safe operation, obstacle riding and rapid dismount.

Walnut Creek takes the mandate of reserve officer bike training one step further by bringing the expertise in-house. Lesser, the reserve sergeant, is a California POST-certified bike instructor.

Pedal Pushers versus Drug Pushers

For those who may denigrate the concept and say that the reserve bike officers offer only window dressing public relations, Mason City's Thomazin points to the use of the bicycles as an enforcement tool which was clearly demonstrated by the Seattle Police Department.

The pedal pushers win when it comes to the war on the drug pushers. "We can cover a lot of distance fast. People don't know we're there until we pop up," he said. "This is a real good tool for drug enforcement."

Whatever the application, be it public relations or narcotics enforcement, the use of reserve officers as bike patrollers is a proven venue for the positive deployment of non-full-time law enforcers.

One reserve bike officer said: "People see us in a different light than when we're sitting in a patrol car handing out lottery tickets to anyone speeding. We can actually stop and talk to them when they're out walking their dog or mowing the lawn."

"People in our community have learned that we're out there and can help," he said. "When they see us coming they wave at us with all their fingers, not just the middle one."

Dr. Richard Weinblatt

April 1996
Law and Order:
The Magazine for Police Management

Reserve Officers Man Boats: Turnover is Low for Police on the 'Baywatch' Beat

"We're so happy with the program that we're looking to expand the use of auxiliary officers," exclaimed Captain Jim Brown, the newly minted state-wide auxiliary and reserve coordinator for the Florida Marine Patrol (FMP).

Known variously as reserves, auxiliaries, specials, and supernumeraries, volunteer and part-time law enforcement personnel have enjoyed an acceptance on the water not often found in other specialized units.

The FMP, which operates under the Florida Department of Environmental Protection, has 363 fully certified officers with state-wide powers spread out over its five districts and 11 field offices. Their responsibilities encompass resource laws as they relate to salt water, boating safety and environmental matters.

Brown said the Florida Marine Patrol's program has seven reserves, mostly former full-time officers, and 90 ("and growing") auxiliaries. The bulk of the auxiliary officers (36) are in the Miami, Broward, and Palm Beach areas.

In Massachusetts, an interesting change in the currents has part-time harbor masters and assistant harbor masters enforcing the laws on the state's waterways. Municipalities with an excess of a certain number of miles of water within its limits may hire part-time officers to act independently from the city police. While some are full-time police officers who do marine duties in addition, many are business people and other residents from the community.

In Hingham, MA, Robert A. Buotte has served as the town's harbor master since 1989. Piloting a 25-foot Boston Whaler boat along 23 miles of shoreline, members of the Harbor Master Department handled 70 search and rescue cases last year, including six errant waterfarers that they saved.

"There are a lot of us," the former Coast Guard commander explained, pointing out that there are over 60 harbor master departments in Massachusetts. As one of the larger harbor master organizations in the state, Hingham pays its ten part-time assistant harbor masters $8.25 an hour.

But no city has more volunteers in uniform than the New York City Police Department. Over 4,000 auxiliary officers serve the mega-agency with 38,500 full-time officers spread out over 76 precincts in the five boroughs. The department even has 17 auxiliaries assigned to the NYPD Harbor unit with a city wide beat which includes the East River, Jamaica Bay, the Hudson Bay, and the Battery.

Speaking from the unit's headquarters at Randall's Island, Officer Brian O'Reilly, the auxiliary coordinator, said that the volunteers patrol in their own vessels as well as a department owned 19 foot Steigercraft. The 14 year law enforcement veteran recalled one wealthy auxiliary officer who conducted his duties from a 63 foot yacht.

"Our auxiliary officers act as the eyes and ears of the police department," said O'Reilly of the group of mostly older, established volunteers. The summer period of May through September comprises the bulk of their far flung water borne activities with weekday hours going from 6:00 PM to 10:00 PM and weekend patrols going all day long.

The 12 members of the Pompton Lakes, NJ, Police Department's Boat Unit have enough business to keep them afloat county-wide. Special Captain Donald K. Meyer, a member of the unit for 21 years, said they go beyond the boundaries of the three-square-mile Passaic County community to "wherever we are needed." The department has 13 full-time officers and the boat detail is staffed by the volunteer officers. Special officers working other duties for the town are paid $12.00 per hour.

Community volunteers built the 1,000-square-foot building alongside police headquarters. The building houses the two 14-foot Sears Game Fisher boats and the Mobile Emergency Command Vehicle. The boats are outfitted with center consoles, 25 horsepower motors, as well as with emergency lights, sirens, radios, and P.A. system.

The Command Center Vehicle, a former Snap-On Tools truck, was purchased with New Jersey Emergency Management funds with the town matching the amount. It has been refurbished with a desk work area inside along with marine, fire department and CB radios, as well as an equipment room and a room to change into scuba gear. The building and the inside of the truck was made possible through donations, fund raisers and the volunteer labor of the officers, their families and the citizens of Pompton Lakes.

Summertime law enforcement activities keeps Illinois' Lake County Sheriff's Police waterborne officers busy. Based out of Waukegan, IL, the 34 part-time deputy sheriffs of the Marine Safety Unit patrol 260 miles of shoreline and have jurisdiction 30 miles (halfway) into Lake Michigan.

"Our people are very happy working on the boats," stated Kurt Proschwitz, Lake County Sheriff's Chief of Operations. The department also has 65 volunteer reservists who undertake other functions and 175 full-time sworn deputy sheriffs to cover the 480 square mile, 560,000 population suburban Chicago county. The part-time marine deputies sail the waters for $9.54 an hour and work from eight to 20 hours per week.

Captain Willie Smith, the Marine Safety Unit commander and a boat owner, said the Sheriff's Police launches their marine deputies on a fleet of ten boats. Lake Michigan has two permanent boats- a 32 foot Boston Whaler and a 28-foot Monarch. Smith said that the unit's equipment is costly, but they have been creative in acquiring some of the necessities from boat companies, including locally based Johnson Motors.

"We patrol the many miles of the very popular inland Chain of Lakes area on Friday and Saturday from 6:00 pm to 2:00 am and weekdays from 6:00 pm to midnight," Smith said. More experienced boat officers police the lake while others work the inland channels area.

Training

As with other duties of reservists, on the job experience alone won't float the boat. Training is emphasized by all of the marine moguls.

"Massachusetts has a new Harbor Masters Academy in Plymouth (MA)," Hingham's Buotte said. "Training will be done in two phases, one beginning in February and the other staring in September." Prior to the 351-hour specialized basic training academy, the part-time marine officers attended the Massachusetts Criminal

Justice Training Council-certified 140 hour reserve/intermittent academy.

The Florida Marine Patrol (FMP), whose program has been in existence for 20 years, looks for their auxiliaries and reserves to obtain state certification. Most of that training is taken through local training facilities with the aspiring volunteer officer picking up the tab.

With the auxiliaries, the base for the certification is 97 hours, although Capt. Brown said most training curriculums average 250 to 300 hours. The FMP has a 240-hour field training officer program for salaried officers, and Brown said they are examining a similar program for auxiliary personnel.

Lake County's Smith said that Illinois recently came up with new minimum standards in January and they are working on how to comply with the new regulations. He said some of the Marine Safety Unit's deputies will be grandfathered into the newly-enhanced certification.

The Pompton Lakes Police Department's boat-borne crew is comprised of one full-time police officer, three Class II. special law enforcement officers (including Meyer), and eight Class I. specials. Meyer said basic training is taken at the Passaic County Police Academy with the Class II.s coming in around the 400-hour mark and 80 hours making up the Class I. training. Class II. special officers carry firearms and have police powers while Class I.s are unarmed and have limited authority.

Pompton Lakes special officers (12 total) take two hours of in-service training each month. Four of the team members are certified scuba divers, while the rest are equipment and/or boat handlers.

The NYPD's O'Reilly said that the auxiliaries in the Harbor Unit are all experienced boaters who train themselves on unit-specific topics during the slower winter months. All of the officers undergo a New York City Police Auxiliary Officer Primary Training Course which is 72 hours in length.

Uniforms

The NYPD provides auxiliary officers with all uniforms and equipment, including an auxiliary harbor unit shoulder patch. Other marine units ask that the officers provide all or part of the attire and accoutrements.

"It runs our officers around $1,500 by the time they are done paying for their training, uniforms, and weapon," observed the Florida Marine Patrol's Brown. Pompton Lakes' newly-minted marine officers purchase their own uniforms initially but receive a $200 annual uniform allowance after the first year. The specials wear the same uniform as the regulars, with the exception of the state-mandated "special law enforcement officer" shoulder patch. Their Sig Saur Model 226 guns are owned by the town.

"We (the special officers) used to have to provide everything, but now the town owns 90% of the scuba and boat equipment," Meyer said. He added that the wet suits are still owned by the individual members of the team.

Getting on Board

With all the action on the water, it's no wonder that getting on board a marine unit is difficult and that turnover is low. Smith said of Lake County's people, "Most have been with us over ten years and some have been here as long as 18 years."

The Florida Marine Patrol has a local auxiliary coordinator in each field office. After prospective auxiliary officers complete the application, an interview follows along with a background investigation, drug screen and physical exam. No polygraph is administered.

New York's Harbor Unit is home to one auxiliary captain, one auxiliary lieutenant, two auxiliary sergeants, and 13 auxiliary officers (APOs). Turnover is low for the volunteers who first set sail in the mid-1960s. The current crew of volunteers must donate at least 20 hours per month and last year put in over 1,500 hours during the May through September period.

O'Reilly said that prospects must meet three criteria: they must have been an auxiliary officer with the NYPD for two years and hold a safety certificate from the U.S. Coast Guard or the U.S. Power Squadron, or they must be able to demonstrate an extensive array of boating knowledge or, lastly, they must have prior military experience in the Navy or Coast Guard.

Pompton Lakes' Meyer, who owns a sporting goods store, said those aspiring to be special officers in his jurisdiction go through an interview process and must attend the county police academy to become either a New Jersey state certified Class I. or Class II. special law enforcement officer (SLEO). He also cited the unit's low turnover.

While many aspects of the water watch may seem appealing, Mayer pointed out that it is not as glamorous as it seems. "When we're called out, it's not under the best of circumstances and often involves looking for bodies," he said. He pointed out that proper cleaning and maintenance of the boating and scuba equipment takes much time and hard work.

Despite the long hours and exposure to sometimes adverse weather conditions, a steady stream of applicants continues to flood the offices of those overseeing marine reserve programs. It is the dedicated service of the volunteer and part-time officers who staff these vital divisions of law enforcement that keep an important public service afloat.

Dr. Richard Weinblatt

September 1996
Law and Order:
The Magazine for Police Management

Reserve Duties Vary in the Bay State: Massachusetts Officers Wear Many Hats

Steeped in the history and tradition of colonial citizen-based policing, non-full-time officers in Massachusetts are continuing to colonize new frontiers. The Bay State's version of reservists are referred to under a variety of names (such as reserve, auxiliary, special, and intermittent), and run under a confusing patchwork of dictated training mandates and duty assignments.

"We have 6,000 volunteer and part-time officers in this state who go from limited roles to very sophisticated duties,' explained Massachusetts Reserve Police Federation president Erick Hoffman. He was referring to the "home rule" concept which drives his state's governmental entities and provides for a very broad application of the reserve officer concept.

Administrative personnel in agencies in Massachusetts also have the influence of very strong union organizations. These unions vary the role of non-full-timers from jurisdiction to jurisdiction. Chiefs and sheriffs do not have to contend with this factor in other parts of the nation.

While the category's classifications are loosely defined by the state, according to Hoffman it is the local department that determines the role played by the officer. Almost all are armed and most are able to work off duty details for pay.

According to Hoffman, auxiliary officers (who are volunteers 90% of the time) are under the old civil defense or emergency management model and have authority while on duty and called out at the discretion of the chief of police or emergency management director. Special officers have an even more varied role, depending on the agency. The chief again determines their duties and whether they have authority off duty. Some towns have auxiliaries who are also sworn in as specials.

Reserve or "permanent intermittent" officers are under civil service and are paid. They take the civil service exam and are placed on the civil service list. Seasonal specials differ in that they are appointed on a yearly basis and are paid during the summer months.

The Massachusetts Criminal Justice Training Council offers a Reserve/Intermittent training course which can be taken by any of the categories at the option of the chief. It's a confusing system to outsiders looking in, yet it seems to work for the law enforcers of Massachusetts.

"The program is great and saves the town $200,000 per year," said Rockland, MA, Police Department chief Kevin M. Donovan. The 30 full-time officer agency located 20 miles south of Boston uses two categories of officers.

The 14 part-time officers are called specials, are civil servants and similar to full-time officers in that they work patrol. They have full police powers and can work road construction jobs, dances and nightclubs to earn extra income at a special detail rate of $33.00 an hour.

The 15 auxiliaries, who are anticipated to go up to 25, serve a one-year probation prior to being appointed specials. The uniforms for the auxiliary and special officers are different from the regular officers. The patch for both officers state "Special Police" and the two Crown Victoria cruisers state "Rockland Aux. Police."

Donovan, who started his career as a reserve/intermittent officer in 1974, said that the caliber of people in his auxiliary/special officer program has risen over the last three years, which has aided in relations with the union.

Chief Thomas E. Burke of West Springfield, MA, echoed his Rockland counterpart's sentiments in stating that his special officers make a difference. The 81 full-time officer agency has 70 specials to work the 17 square mile town located 90 miles west of Boston.

"We hire another 60 specials during the Big E (Eastern States Exposition) to work for $14.00 an hour on three shifts in what amounts to be a small city," the chief explained. He said that the 17-day event taxes his agency and the specials provide police services for the over one million visitors to the exposition.

The Big E pays the specials and a local dealership loans minivans to patrol the grounds. He said that the additional help is sworn in a week before the event.

Finding themselves in a similar boat, only this time for the whole summer, is the 91 full-time officer Barnstable, MA, Police in Cape Cod, where the population swells from 43,000 to 110,000 in the summer. Responsible for 64 square miles and seven villages (including the tony enclaves of Hyannis and Hyannis Port), administrative sergeant Richard L. Howard said that they could not do it without the addition of 21 seasonal officers who assist with walking beats and traffic control, as well as with the three marine patrol units.

Howard said that the seasonals, who are paid $10.00 an hour, come back year after year from June 1 to September 13 to help them with 38,000 calls for police service. They are folks such as criminal justice students and mature school teachers who have time in the summer to work Cape Cod's ritzy law enforcement beat.

Howard said that the Barnstable Police Department makes sure that the seasonal officers get over 100 hours of training and are reserve/intermittent certified.

West Springfield's Burke said that many small towns are prepared to meet the liability concern head on and that his agency trains extensively. His specials attend the regional academy at Agawam, MA, for 16 weeks at night and a few Saturdays. They also get 40 hours of in-service training annually.

Rockland also ensures Massachusetts state certification through the 200-hour reserve/intermittent program at the Plymouth Police Academy, which is held for 20 weeks at night and covers the usual fare including firearms. That's particularly important to Rockland's Donovan as he pointed out that his officers are in the process of switching from Glock .9mm to Glock .40 caliber handguns.

Donovan said that to get to the training (and ultimately to the streets of Rockland), the prospective part-time law enforcer fills out a detailed 25-page application. A background investigation is conducted, including credit check. A pre-screening auxiliary oral board takes place with a chief's interview following. Barnstable has a similar gauntlet of applications with oral boards and medical checkups following.

With the Massachusetts Reserve Law Enforcement Federation's figure of 6,000 citizens involved in law enforcement, the Bay State ranks as one of the highest states in the nation for reserve type policing. Hoffman, who oversees a membership of 1,500, reflected on the large numbers: "We fully expect that the reserve concept will continue to grow in Massachusetts."

Dr. Richard Weinblatt

Dr. Richard Weinblatt

December 1996
Law and Order:
The Magazine for Police Management

Advice for Reserves: The Reserves' Legal Eagles and Insurance Icons Weigh In

Much as full-time officers are facing an increasingly complex calling fraught with legal and insurance woes, so too are the many men and women who perform law enforcement services on a volunteer or part-time compensated basis. These officers are known variously as reserve, auxiliary, special or supernumerary.

This column explores the issues that reservists should be concerned with by consulting directly with an array of legal and insurance experts across the nation who themselves are also serving as reserve officers.

"While reserves should not be paranoid, they ought to know what they can do," opined Robert A. Sneed, a noted attorney in Atlanta, GA, who serves as a fully

Georgia POST state certified Reserve Deputy with the Fulton County Sheriff's Department's Training Division. He added that if the reserve is too paranoid concerning legal issues, he or she "should get out of being a reserve."

Howard Ekerling, a Sherman Oaks, CA, attorney and 14-year veteran Level I-designated reserve officer with the Los Angeles Police Department, said that many reserves earn more from their regular jobs than salaried officers do and generally have larger homes and other assets that could be attached. "We have quite a few lawyers serving as reserves in the LAPD," Ekerling pointed out. "If the risk was that great, you'd think lawyers would be the first to know and get out of being a reserve officer."

While the expensive house that Ekerling referred to may be a ripe target, all those interviewed felt that elaborate asset protection devices such as trusts were overkill. A more appropriate protection involves attention to training issues. Sneed, who also serves as a recorder's and municipal court judge, and the others interviewed stressed that training and knowledge of applicable laws, legal precedents and departmentally promulgated policies are the key considerations that keep a reserve officer out of trouble.

"Training takes care of the liability," advised Sneed who felt that training pursuits should replace unnecessary litigation worrying. "Make sure you get training at the department and, if they don't have any, seek it out on your own. Then keep good records."

Sneed, who holds a bachelor's degree in criminal justice and the Juris Doctor as well as a Master's (LL.M.) in litigation, has served as a reserve deputy sheriff since 1993 and enjoys serving the community. He felt that reserves may be a bit more of a target since the "reserve by nature is in another profession." He said that it is incumbent on the diligent reservist to make sure that he or she "knows the job as well or better than any full-timer."

Ekerling echoed the concept. Stressing that a certain amount of legal awareness is healthy for anyone in the law enforcement field, the graduate of the UCLA School of Law pointed out that "anyone can be sued for anything" and that a reserve officer is as ripe a candidate for such litigation action as any other litigation target. Even so, sleepless nights are an extreme reaction.

Sneed pointed out that certain reserves may be more apt to be sued than others depending on their function. He said that a reserve working warrants, where there is a lot of physical contact, is more vulnerable than a reserve working in the station's insular office environment.

Certain states, such as Ohio, provide a modicum of protection for volunteer and part-time officers – provided that they are fully certified by the state law enforcement officer certification body. Non-certified volunteer officers in Ohio are not covered under the statute and thus are in a much more precarious and vulnerable position.

"Certified officers, regardless of status, are covered under statute as long as they stay within the guidelines and policies of their agency," explained Howard Mellon, a private practice attorney in the Columbus, OH, area who serves as a part-time paid officer with the Miflin Township, OH, Police Department. He explained that the statute requires an act of "gross negligence and willful and wanton misconduct" in order for it to be litigated. He said that it is a higher standard than that applied in other states such as Illinois.

The state of Alabama, on the other hand, provides some protection to reserves as long as they are not paid. The law is applied in a manner roughly akin to the Good Samaritan laws. Part-time officers apparently are not afforded such statutory peace of mind. Ekerling, who also serves as general counsel for the powerful California Reserve Peace Officers Association (CRPOA), said that if a conflict arises between the governmental entity and the reservist, the tenant/homeowner insurance policy may provide some measure of assistance.

"An intentional tort is probably defensible," said Ekerling, who recommended at least a million dollar umbrella insurance policy. "The carrier may not be indemnified, but they may have a duty to defend on a lawsuit if a conflict arises between the city and the reserve officer.

Attorney Mellon agreed that it would behoove the prudent reserve to look into "buying a lot of insurance."

He said that a visit to the insurance agent is in order. Sneed said that a standard homeowners' policy may not cover the situation adequately and a separate rider may be in order. He also strongly advised that reserves consult with insurance professionals.

So we did.

Lee F. Pamplin, executive director of the Alabama Sheriffs Reserve Association and a long-time insurance executive, said that reserves should ask their insurance agent about an all risk coverage homeowners' policy which is referred to in Alabama as a "Form Five."

Much in the vein of Ohio's statutory protection, Pamplin said that some insurance companies may hinge coverage of a reserve based on whether they are considered employees. He cited as an example Alabama where the state does not recognize a reserve's actions unless they are state certified or under the direct supervision of a certified reserve or full-time officer. He said that it is open to interpretation as to whether radio contact supervision is adequate.

Pamplin, who has donned a reserve deputy uniform for years, said that one question to ask the agent is if a business auto and emergency vehicle endorsement is in order. Reflecting on the trend of many reserves to use their personal cars for police-related business, Papmlin said this is an area often overlooked. He said an inexpensive endorsement may cover that critical area.

Joe Patton, owner of the Patton Insurance Agency in Tacoma, WA, and a Pierce County Sheriff's Department reserve deputy for eight years, said that even with a homeowners policy, a reserve could be liable and be personally sued. He, in line with the others interviewed, felt that a department should cover the reserve as agency guidelines were followed.

Patton said that a reserve's main concern "should be how does the department protect us in terms of death and disability." He explained that in the state of Washington, each governmental entity now has the opportunity to approve a state passed act that provides modest retirement benefits that may especially be useful in the event of injury.

"Pierce County just approved the plan where each reserve deputy sheriff pays $30.00 per year and the county kicks in an additional $70.00," Patton explained. "After ten years, the reserve can pull out a small retirement."

Such was not the case in 1985 when two rural county reserve deputies were shot. Tragically, one was killed and the other was permanently disabled, causing the Association of County Commissions of Alabama's (ACCA) fund to pay out workers' compensation to the tune of $750,000. The incident put the ACCA out of the reserve arena, though they still pay $18,000 per annum to the Liberty Mutual Assigned Risk Pool. Pamplin said that the Alabama Sheriffs Reserve Association was created in 1985 primarily to handle claims.

Many independent state reserve associations, such as the Texas Reserve Law Officers Association and the California Reserve Peace Officers Association, have long had programs which provide benefits to member reserves in cases of death or injury.

The legal and insurance situations that reserves find themselves in on a regular basis across the country has led many state reserve associations to take further action. James C. Lombardi, president of the CRPOA and reserve officer in charge of the Los Angeles Police Department said that he and Howard Ekerling are in the midst of creating a state-wide list of lawyers who are also reserve officers to serve as defense representatives for their fellow reservists.

With a concerted effort in the area of bona fide training and intelligent questions posed to insurance and legal professionals, the typical reserve officer should be able to go about his or her service to the community in an unfettered manner.

Dr. Richard Weinblatt

April 1997
Law and Order:
The Magazine for Police Management

Rank Insignia for Reserves: Debate Revolves Around Public Perception and Officer Acceptance

Few topics in the arena of reserve or auxiliary police officers are more controversial than that of visible rank insignia for such personnel.

On one side of the fence are those who believe that reserves should be composed of various ranks and reflect those status positions via collar insignia and the like. On the other side are people who subscribe to the theory that such a display of rank, and the accompanying issues, creates problems for reserves who are striving to fit in even under ideal circumstances.

"The use of ranks for reserve officers is confusing for the public and breeds ill will by the regular officers," said Don McMullan, the incognito Captain of Reserves for the Houston County Sheriff's Department. The agency is based in Dothan, AL, located in the southeast corner of Alabama by the Georgia and Florida border.

According to McMullan, who has served the 50 full-time deputy agency since 1970, the department had previously displayed rank in the form of collar insignia on the reserves who sport the same uniform, gun and other equipment as the regulars. The 40-member reserve contingent of both state certified and non-certified law enforcers includes a captain (McMullan), one lieutenant and two sergeants.

"When a ranked reserve officer rode with a regular deputy, people sometimes bypassed the full-time officer to speak with who they viewed as the ranking officer on the scene," McMullan said. "We wanted to eliminate the barriers that sometimes exist between reserves and deputies."

Terry Latin, president of the Washington State Reserve Law Officers Association and a 28 year veteran Seattle Police Department reserve officer, said he has long held that ranks should be present "only on paper, not in the field."

Lattin contended that is confusing. "Ranks just drive a wedge between the regulars and the reserves that we don't need," he said. "In Seattle, we never had them and we don't need them."

Dr. Richard Weinblatt

The third-term reserve association president recalled an incident in a nearby suburb of Seattle in which a complainant on a call for police service walked right by the full-time officer and started talking to the rank-strewn reserve. "The full-time cop got a little upset and yelled: 'Hey, talk to me. That guy's just a reserve,'" Lattin said.

An even more disconcerting situation was reported by a central Florida sheriff's agency. According to the reserve liaison who coordinates that large department's program, a full-time patrol deputy was joined by his best friend: a reserve sergeant. A citizen at a traffic stop was upset with the full-timer's demeanor and requested to speak with his supervisor. The deputy steered the irate man to "his sergeant" accompanying him. Not satisfied with the reserve sergeant's handling of the matter, the frustrated man took his concerns to the Sheriff's Department's headquarters.

"It soon came out what had transpired in the field," said the reserve officer who requested anonymity for himself and his agency. "Needless to say, we do not have ranks apparent to the public in our reserve program anymore."

Many departments, such as Houston County, have ranks but keep them out of the public eye. "The ranks are just for internal administrative purposes," McMullan said.

In Seattle, the 50-officer reserve force is uniformed and armed identically to regular officers, with the reserve structure apparent only on organizational charts and internal memos. For years, the Los Angeles Police

Department set the trend for the non-intrusive rank approach with its officer-in-charge, James C. Lombardi, donning the uniform of an LAPD patrol officer.

Houston County's McMullan reported that the change made by Sheriff Lamar Glover has eased tensions and lessened public confusion for the agency which serves an 85,000 population county 95 miles North of Panama City, FL. Unfortunately, as is often the case in government, change does not come easily and many factors enter into the equation.

In New Jersey a few years back, an auxiliary lieutenant recognized that the presence of a volunteer officer reserve structure in the suburban police department was creating problems with the full-time officers. He offered to relinquish the visible accoutrements, retaining only the internal recognition for his position but his suggestion was rebuffed by the full-time administrative structure. The reasoning offered for the denial was that others of rank in the auxiliary force would take such a stripping as an insult.

Another agency, this one in the Southwest, after the installation of a new reserve liaison, successfully made the switch for just such reasons previously noted. Unfortunately, the Sheriff's Department lost the reserve captain who took the removal of the collar bars as a "demotion" rather than a change in the uniform. Attempts to convince him of the true nature of the change were unsuccessful, and he resigned.

Interestingly, there appears to be a corresponding lack of respect that reserves have in a given region and the propensity for a rank laden reserve hierarchy. In metropolitan areas, such as Chicago, New York City and Washington, DC, where reserves are often differentiated from the full-timers in their duties and sometimes even in their uniforms, the volunteer officers often look to the display of gold as a shoring up of their status.

Many lower ranked reserves and full-timers have a different take on the scene. The visible ranks, particularly when the volunteer officer program in question delineates vast differences in the duties of full-timers and reservists, become a post less serious than what their bearers would like to think of them as.

"We see these auxiliary captains, (auxiliary) deputy inspectors and (auxiliary) inspectors walking around giving orders to auxiliary officers when they don't know the first thing about real police work," said one progressive-thinking New York City Police Department officer. He, like others when faced with this controversial topic, requested anonymity. "It looks like they are playing 'commander,'" he said.

The college-educated NYPD officer is open-minded enough to point out that he has no problem with the equally screened, equally trained and deployed concept of reserves being embraced throughout the nation. His concern is the use of similarly uniformed, much lesser-trained volunteers who operate as an almost separate entity from the NYPD regulars, but sport rank insignia that confuses the public and acts as a bully pulpit to feed the ego.

In defense, the administration of the approximately 40,000 full-time officer New York City Police Department has long contended that their program's rank structure is crucial to the overseeing of an auxiliary officer program which has more than 4,000 volunteer officers spread out over 76 precincts covering the five boroughs of the city.

In the nation's other large city at the opposite coast, James C. Lombardi, the Los Angeles Police Department's reserve officer in charge, does not run into such problems as his program is fully integrated into the regular officer structure. Reservists are not primarily deployed on duties separate from the regulars as they are in New York City.

The use of reserve ranks, long a tradition in the Northeast U.S. where volunteer policing hails back to the era of civil defense, is increasingly eschewed by agencies striving to ensure that their volunteer or part-time officers are serving for altruistic, non-ego related reasons. Further, they hope that such a policy encourages cooperation between full-timers and part-timers and minimizes confusion for the public.

Dr. Richard Weinblatt

June 1997
Law and Order:
The Magazine for Police Management

Riding with Reserve FTOs: Field Training Programs Vary in Different Departments for Reserve Officer Recruits

Just as the type of volunteer and part-time police officers vary across the nation, so too does the implementation of FTO programs for the reserve component of an agency. Some volunteer officers find themselves under the tutelage of full-time officers, while other (more traditional) programs have the reserve rookies paired up with more senior reservists.

"We only recently came up with a formal written program governing new reserve officers and the improvements showed," said Paramus, NJ, Police Reserve Lieutenant Frank Rizzo. Rizzo is the architect of a sophisticated volunteer officer FTO program for the

24-reserve officer contingent located 10 miles west of New York City.

Rizzo, who serves as president of the New Jersey Auxiliary Police Officers Association, explained that the void of reserve or auxiliary officer FTO program is a situation present in many of the Garden State's volunteer police organizations.

Paramus pairs new reserves with trained FTOs who themselves are reserves. The FTO stint, based loosely on several programs including those used by the San Jose, CA, and Portsmouth, VA Police Departments, lasts a minimum of 18 tours of duty (one tour a week) and a minimum of six months. Exceptions are only made in the case of a lateral reserve or auxiliary officer transfer from another New Jersey agency.

Paramus volunteer officers ply their duties in a highly congested suburban environment assisting the 89 full-time officers. Rizzo explained that the first two shifts serve as an introduction during which time the trainee watches. From tour number three on, the FTO starts to fade into the background and becomes the second officer.

"We play out scenarios en route to the call utilizing the concept of contact and cover. There are times, if the call is more complicated, that the FTO steps forward to take the lead," Rizzo said. He added that all participants in the program must have completed the academy prior to starting with an FTO.

In Washington State just North of Seattle, newly elected Sheriff Rick Bart, an FBI National Academy graduate, has his fully sworn reserve deputy sheriffs complete a six month FTO program riding with a senior reservist.

The reserve deputies- who take the same oath and are uniformed and armed the same as full-timers- complete a 240-hour, in-house reserve academy over the course of four months and enter the FTOM program within the reserve structure. They are required to ride a minimum of 16 hours per month.

The Durham, NC, Police Department, in keeping with North Carolina law, mandates that its 35 reserve officers be fully state-certified graduates of a minimum 480-hour basic law enforcement training (BLET) academy. The aspiring reservists pay their own way through a community college training system, and Durham culls their reserves from the local Durham Technical Community College. What follows is a rigorous two-year program riding with full-time FTOs.

"They (new reserves) are assigned to a squad, but not to a particular officer," explained Staff Sergeant J.W. Piatt, the reserve liaison, who himself is a former reserve. "For the first six months, they ride only with full-time line FTO officers." During that initial period, the reserve officer has to put in a minimum of 16 hours per month with at least eight hours monthly service required thereafter.

Bridging the Gap Between Reserve and Regular

The Santa Fe County Sheriff's Department in Santa Fe, NM, is currently evolving its reserve deputy FTO program and has recently paired two of its reserves with a full-time Patrol Division deputy for field training. While the process for the reserves has been enhanced, a side benefit has accrued.

"Putting a reserve with a full-time deputy FTO helps to get over some of the jealousies and other petty problems that exist between reserves and regulars and happen everywhere to some extent," said Santa Fe County Sheriff Benjamin L. Montano. "We all have an equal chance to get killed out there, whether reserve or not, and I want us all to be one."

"In addition to learning more, I feel more a part of the shift and work closer with the (full-time) deputies," said Reserve Deputy Russell A. Schweiger, whose full-time occupation is as a social worker for the State of New Mexico. The integrated FTO program approach has facilitated his socializing with the regulars after work.

Reserve Deputy Raymond G. Zamora, a full-time state corrections officer, chimed in that he "gets the best calls, which helps in picking up the job quicker." The County's dispatchers often utilize the two-man status of the FTO/reserve car for violent domestic disputes and the like. Other cars are one man units.

Patrol Sergeant Stacy S. Saiz, whose shift has been the beneficiary of the two reserve trainees' donated manpower, said he's seen a difference of having them work with a regular deputy. "They seem more confident knowing that they've been taught by a person who does this complicated job day in and day out," Saiz said. "That in turn helps the department, especially when they will be released to handle calls on their own."

But getting released in high-expectation agencies is no easy feat. Demands placed on the new reserves are often greater than the time required of veteran volunteers due to the concern for the learning curve.

The Durham Police Department, which doubles the normal eight-hours-per-month requirement during the first six months, mandates that the trainee take a blank evaluation form with him or her for each shift. The filled out form is sent to the reserve supervisor. After serving for two years as a Durham police reserve with full-time officers and at least four reserve commanders, as well as getting four full-time FTO recommendations, the aspiring solo officer's packet is reviewed by the command staff that pass final judgment.

Snohomish County reserves, who serve in the state's third largest sheriff's department, are evaluated each shift and have an additional monthly overall evaluation. At the end of the six-month period, the full-time deputy and full-time lieutenant (who oversee the 50 reserves), along with three seasoned reserves, sit down and evaluate the write-ups.

"Once they've been released, our reserves can ride together or with a full-time deputy," said Sheriff Bart. His 180 full-time deputies average 992 calls annually.

While discharging the minimum 18 shifts and at least six months, during which time the trainee brings their copy of the FTO program, the Paramus Police Department's reserve FTOs fill out a two sided single sheet evaluation form which indicates performance in such areas as vehicle operations, patrol operations, report writing and the like.

The original is kept by the trainee with a copy kept by the assigned FTO. After the six month process is completed, they ride with two reserve supervisors, who also evaluate them, and a written test is taken.

"We grade them on a one to ten scale with ten being the highest," said Rizzo who noted that there is also a "not observed" notation available. "After everything is successfully done, they move off probation to reserve officer 3rd class rank. Other options available include remedial training, extended probation or dismissal.

The Santa Fe County Sheriff's Department has the full-time deputy complete a typed three page evaluation of the reserve each shift. This is reviewed by the shift sergeant and given to the reserve administration. Because of the busy nature of the agency, no absolute time limit has been put on the reserve deputies to get released for solo patrol. The county uniforms and arms its reserve deputies exactly like the regulars, and some volunteers are assigned take-home marked patrol cars.

Crucial to the success of any FTO program for volunteer or part-time officers is the officers doing the field training. Along with the requisite qualities of patience, an intimate knowledge of law enforcement and the credibility of experience, FTOs should set an example that illustrates excellence.

While these qualities, particularly experience, are more easily come by with full-timers, programs that do utilize their reserves as FTOs should monitor the situation closely and take advantage of any outside training available.

In 1994, the New Jersey Auxiliary Police Officers Association's Training Academy sponsored a 24-hour University of Delaware "Certified Police Field Training Officer" course at its South Brunswick Township, NJ, facility and four of Paramus' volunteer finest, including Rizzo, graduated from the program. "Only University of Delaware-certified FTOs can work in that capacity, which ensures that our program has credibility and is effective," explained Rizzo who works full-time as a printing company president in Jersey City, NJ. "That is the standard we have for all future FTOs."

The maintenance of high standards, whether the FTO in question is a full-time officer or a reservist, is the key to the shaping of a reserve patrol officer.

Dr. Richard Weinblatt

April 1998
Law and Order:
The Magazine for Police Management

Special Deputy Marshal Myths Busted

In the quest for non-full-time posts perceived to be glamorous, some local reserve and auxiliary officers have inquired as to opportunities to serve on the federal level as a Special Deputy United States Marshal. Much of the desire to don the five pointed pentacle star may be pinned on the imagination-invoking history of the United States Marshal in our nation's old west history, which is rooted in misconceptions. This column is geared to answering the queries and busting the myths surrounding these little known and enigmatic federal crime busters.

Founded in 1789, this oldest federal law enforcement agency used to rely heavily on part-time deputies who were poorly screened and ill-trained. The United States Marshals Service (USMS) has clearly moved away from that simplistic part-time personnel management approach in a manner reflective of its complex modern day role in federal criminal justice services.

There are 94 presidentially appointed United States Marshals, around 2,600 full-time deputy U.S. marshals, and some 1,200 civilian administrative support personnel. This multi-faceted arm of the U.S. Department of Justice is responsible for federal level fugitive investigations, court security, prisoner transportation, witness security protection and other duties as directed by the attorney general and the federal judiciary. But even with those numbers, the USMS is stretched by its many different hats, and special deputies augment the workforce.

According to Robert C. Leschorn, chief inspector and team leader of the Executive Services Division for the United States Marshals Service and the agency's guru on the special deputy program, the post has evolved into one that is tightly controlled and monitored. No longer are special deputy U.S. marshal commissions doled out as they once were.

"The days of someone being a commercial pilot by night and a special deputy marshal by day are just about over," Leschorn stated emphatically from Marshals Service headquarters in Arlington, Virginia. He was eager to break the stereotypes some have of the part-time federal officers and to clarify how and when they are utilized in the 94 federal districts.

Special deputy U.S. marshals are sworn in for a year's time and their federal commission must be renewed annually to remain valid. Leschorn said that the Marshals Service received and approved 579 requests in 1997 covering some 3,500 individuals.

Contrary to popular belief, according to Leschorn, most of those commissioned are persons already affiliated with law enforcement who are serving in municipal, county or state capacities. They must hold up under Justice Department scrutiny which includes law enforcement academy or P.O.S.T. state certification and current qualification with firearms. Additionally, in accordance with the Lautenberg Amendment, no domestic violence record can exist.

Once these hurdles are cleared, newly minted special deputies find themselves assisting the feds with court security or guarding prisoners. These persons have authority only while on duty and turn in their credentials and weapon upon leaving the work site. However, a number of them are on task forces or work for the local U.S. Marshal's district office on a part-time basis for extra income.

Contract Court Security

The more visible component of the specially deputized elite, distinctly clad in blue blazers and gray pants, are full-time contract court security officers (CSO), who present the first line of defense for our nation's federal judiciary. The numbers of these persons, who are governed under a national contract, is larger than many would initially realize. For example, the Eastern District of Arkansas has 20 of these folks screening those entering federal court.

Contract security personnel, replete with their special deputy status, even work at the U.S. Marshals Service headquarters. These individuals, like many others throughout the country, have law enforcement or military police experience.

Detention Officers

Some of the larger districts' Marshals Offices employ detention officers who serve as guards in the cell blocks. These people are full-timers with the United States Marshals Service and they are afforded full employment benefits. The special deputy status allows them to conduct their duties unfettered.

"We have 15 detention officers who free up our deputies," said Tony Perez, chief deputy U.S. marshal for the Central District of California in Los Angeles.

Task Forces

"We'll grant special deputy status to qualified state and local law enforcement officers who exhibit a need to expand boundaries in the fight against violent crime," Leschorn explained. He elaborated that the special deputization confers limited powers to enforce laws and carry firearms across state lines. The status is 24 hour in nature, but is limited by the life of the task force assignment.

The Marshals Service and the Deputy Attorney General overseeing the program examine each locally promulgated request closely. Among the situations that have seen requests granted have been officers involved in inter-state investigations pertaining to violent crime, wiretap and electronic interchange, as well as personal and property protection.

"We had a situation where very valuable paintings were moved to the Smithsonian Institution. Local police officers needed to protect the paintings, so a short term special deputy certification was arranged," Leschorn said.

In the Eastern District of Arkansas, U.S. Marshal Conrad Pattillo has ten local officers deputized and functioning as task force members.

The Southern District of Texas has a very active task force contingent filled with local officers imbued with federal authority. Deputy U.S. Marshal Eric Wallenius, public affairs officer for the federal district based in Houston, said that their Gulf Coast Violent Offenders Task Force includes representatives from the Houston Police Department, Harris County Sheriff's Department, Montgomery County Sheriff's Department and the Texas Department of Public Safety (DPS).

In addition to the standard task forces, the Marshal's Office for the Central District of California has 15 local officers teamed with full-time deputy U.S. marshals in a unique outfit dubbed Equal Justice. The majority are from the California Department of Justice, though others hail from the Los Angeles Police Department and area law enforcement agencies.

"These state and local officers work with us to look for fugitives," said Tony Perez, chief deputy of the busy Los Angeles-based district. "We join and help them (the locals) to look for their fugitives as well. The teamwork helps to suppress local crimes as federal fugitives often commit them too."

Part-time Income

Leschorn pointed out that while the United States Marshals Service is using fewer part-timers, the need to augment full-time manpower exists. He said that the average of 27,000 prisoners in custody each day necessitates the use of intermittent paid personnel.

"Some 95% of these special deputies are sworn (local) law enforcement officers looking to make extra money," he commented. He said that each district's U.S. Marshal makes the hourly wage rate determination. As part-timers, the special deputies are not granted any employee benefits. At the federal court in Washington, DC, the rate paid special deputy U.S. marshals has been pegged by that district at $15.00 per hour. "We have a long list of local officers who can augment our forces and we pay in the $16.00 (an hour) range," said the Houston Marshals Office's Eric Wallenius. "Officers working here are not given an actual ID as special deputies, but they do have federal authority for the shift they work.

Another policy which varies between federal districts is whether those employed are retired law enforcers or are current serving as full-time police officers, sheriff's deputies or state troopers.

Tom Bustamante, chief deputy for the district of New Mexico based in Albuquerque, New Mexico, said he has a need for local agencies to assist, but that agencies in the region prohibit the practice.

Texas has looser regulations and officers can work for us part-time. Here we use retired officers due to the restrictions," Bustamante said. He added that his office was trying to "to get away from the shadow work force."

Other districts, such as Perez' Central District of California and Pattillo's Eastern District of Arkansas, may use local officers with the proviso that the aspiring special deputy's agency approves. Pattillo, however, has run into a different kind of problem than local administrative constraints.

"In the Little Rock area, officers have greater opportunities working for local businesses and don't work for us. I mostly get officers from smaller agencies or outlying areas," Pattillo said.

One state officer who has reaped the rewards of extra income through his special deputy U.S. marshal stints is Arkansas State Police trooper first class Rick Newton. He started working for Pattillo in 1993. "When the full-time deputy marshals had to protect the abortion clinics, part-time deputies were needed to handle the courtroom and prisoner security duties. Our State Police Colonel, John Bailey, sent out a formal letter to the troopers saying that the Marshal was shorthanded and that working for them was approved," Newton said.

Newton, who is based out of the State Police's Troop D headquarters in Forrest City, Arkansas, has worked every type of USMS duty from fugitive investigation to courtroom security. He has also conducted numerous prisoner transports both in state and out of state to such locales as Oklahoma, Tennessee and Texas. His deputy hours range from 24 hours to 80 hours per month.

"I send the Marshal my schedule each month and they're very accommodating. The money has made my life more comfortable," Newton said. He added that the arrangement has the benefit of making a better working relationship between the agencies. "I may work under their policies and guidelines, but they learn from us as well."

Special deputy United States marshals today do not dovetail into the image that many have. Such a picture is a misconception more reflective of the easily garnered star badge of yester-year.

Rather, the modern special deputy U.S. marshal is reflective of the complex and professional mission orientation of the United States Marshals Service. In the spirit of reserve type officers, special deputies augment their full-time federal deputy brethren. Their service bridges the gap and promotes understanding between different types of law enforcers.

Dr. Richard Weinblatt

November/December 1999
Corrections Technology & Management

So You Want to Be a Volunteer Probation Officer

Two years ago, Thomas and Carrie Sunday decided to fight boredom in a way that would not be contemplated by most couples. Even the most civic-minded of people would not envision a marriage with the nuptial activities undertaken by the two Tennesseans.

The Sundays each spent in excess of 1,500 hours per year in the toughest most dangerous neighborhoods in Memphis. Armed with nothing more than the badge of an auxiliary probation officer and their persistent drive to make a difference in young people's lives, they tread where few married people would.

Quite a few progressive probation departments are discharging their part of the corrections component by using volunteers in a newly stepped up manner to augment their case-laden staffs. This is a hands-on situation that involves more than just making photocopies in the office.

"I am impressed that we get people who care about their community. We are fortunate that we have such wonderful people," said Bobbie B. Higgins, the coordinator of Auxiliary Probation Services for the Memphis and Shelby County Juvenile Court. She counts the Sundays among the 300 auxiliary probation officers (APOs) she supervises.

"Kids are our future and we have to do this. Someone has to deal with them," said an impassioned Thomas Sunday who, along with his wife, was recently was honored with a plaque designating them as auxiliary probation officer of the year in Shelby County.

Thomas Sunday was himself a troubled youngster who managed to get on the right track. He went into the U.S. Army, served in Vietnam with Special Forces, and settled into a successful career as an architect. This is his way to serve as a positive role model for those who have no guidance.

The couple's journey into some of Memphis' most troubled homes began more than two years ago. Thomas Sunday thought that his wife was getting bored staying at home. When he saw a recruitment pamphlet for the auxiliary probation officer program he showed it to her. They ended up both donating their time.

"We are mentors who also have a responsibility for the courts," said Thomas Sunday who, along with his wife

Carrie, was recently appointed to the Persistent Offender juvenile gang task force.

"If you're not part of the solution, than you're part of the problem," echoed Carrie Sunday. "It's wonderful. I feel like I'm helping."

"We started our program in 1992. We had volunteers, but my predecessor wanted to do more and so the associate probation officer program was born," said Dennis Williams, a probation officer III. and the coordinator of the initiative for the San Bernardino County, California, Probation Department. He said the agency won an award from the National Association of Counties (NAC) in recognition of the program.

"Resources are slim and we have to do more with less," said Gerard N. Bergeron, a deputy probation officer nad volunteer probation officer (VPO) coordinator for the Orange County, California, Probation Department. The department employs more than 300 full-time deputy probation officers and has 46 active volunteer probation officers.

The six-year veteran probation officer said that the volunteer probation officers extend the reach of the full-timers in his department who supervise a daunting caseload.

The 80-year-old department supervises in excess of 13,000 adults and 6,000 juveniles. The average adult caseload runs at 125 with the juvenile caseload coming in at 75. The agency also operates four juvenile institutions that house some 800 juvenile offenders.

In the probation business, time is money- and lives. Orange County volunteers must serve the Santa Ana-based agency at least 20 hours per month for a minimum of one year.

Higgins said Shelby County's 300 highly involved auxiliary probation officers handle a minimum of two cases each with some auxiliaries handling three to four cases. A few standouts, such as Thomas Sunday, take on seven cases. Each case involves one home visit and three telephone contacts every week and, as many full-time probation professionals know, the accompanying mountain of paperwork.

"I just don't know how these folks can handle the caseload and a full-time job," said Higgins who added that some volunteers in her organization have been at it for 20 years. Two people have been carrying the APO badge and juvenile court identification card for 25 years.

Higgins said that the auxiliaries end up donating more than just their time. Expenses, such as gas, come from the volunteers' own pocket.

Like Orange County, the San Bernardino County, California, Probation Department requires their associate probation officers to work 20 hours per month of voluntary duty. Some expenses are reimbursed.

"We really utilize these people in many of the facets of the job," said Williams of the agency's 85 active member volunteer officer program. The department has 150 full-time probation officers.

Duties

Just as the titles vary, so too do the duties of volunteer probation officers. Some agencies have them operating in a sworn capacity carrying badges and fulfilling the same responsibilities as full-time probation officers. Others take a more restrictive role citing training, experiential, labor, or liability issues.

"Our auxiliary probation officers are sworn officers of the court. They can place a violation against the child and can make referrals to children's services," said Higgins who said they act as the eyes and ears of the court and make reports.

Under the Memphis/Shelby County setup, APOs supervise two programs. The "Bypass" intervention program is concerned with children under 14 involved in lesser offenses. The "Supervised" program steps the APO up to situations where the juveniles are deemed delinquent and the cases are more serious.

"My wife and I work out of Division Ten (county-wide) and take the worst cases. We deal with kids involved in drive-bys, assaults, burglaries, and sexual assault," said Thomas Sunday who observed that female juvenile offenders today are a lot more violent and difficult to handle than their male counterparts.

Both Orange County and San Bernardino County have taken a slightly more restrictive stance with their deployment of volunteer officer personnel.

"Volunteer probation officers here do not have arrest powers. We don't use them in enforcement activities," said Orange County's Bergeron. The county details explicitly what their volunteer probation officers can and cannot do.

Volunteer probation officers in Orange County are restricted from participating in arrests, handcuffing, or search and seizure activities either with deputized staff or on their own. They also do not have the final word on casework decisions or preparation of documents to court or case files.

They cannot be involved in urinalysis testing in the field or handling pupilometer exams. They are also prohibited from engaging in in-custody transporting of probationers or unaccompanied home calls at night when they are solo.

They are allowed to handle school contacts for juvenile probationers, adult or juvenile in-custody interviews and urinalysis in area offices.

Bergeron explained that their VPOs can do home visits once a full-time probation officer has checked the household out and a supervisor's approval has been garnered.

"We stopped home visits around February of 1998 due to concerns and on-going discussions here in the office. San Bernardino is an active area and these good people are not peace officers under P.C. 832," said Williams referring to the California statute that defines sworn personnel.

Williams recalled that 30 associate probation officers had worked in the field prior to the home visits prohibition edict and that they never had an incident. He said the debate started with the topic of issuing O.C. pepper spray.

"Do we issue pepper spray to them? If so, do we train them? Even those who were previously trained had to be trained by us per liability," said Williams who added that reports are always reviewed by a supervisor.

Even with the restrictions, associate probation officers are extremely involved in the workings of the probation department.

In the agency's drug diversion unit, the volunteers conduct intake and assessments to determine whether the candidate meets the criteria for the program.

Other associate probation officers assist in case management and some have worked themselves up to putting together major elements of pre-sentence reports or disposition documents.

"One lady in our Juvenile Division developed and implemented a petty theft diversion program in the

Valley. Her work became a successful program," recalled Williams.

Recruitment and Training

Quality recruitment and training is an integral part of a good reserve or auxiliary probation officer program. Higgins said that her office in Memphis has recruitment and training at the top of their agenda.

"We are constantly recruiting and we have constant attrition due to the heart wrenching, long-term commitment," said Higgins. She said they have a turnover rate of around 100 to 125 people per annum.

San Bernardino has an active program that sees a lot of college students participating.

"The students like to see if they like the job as a career and can maybe get their foot in the door. Over 90 have been hired from our program into corrections or law enforcement jobs. We've hired 60 of the 90," said Williams proudly. He added that they don't stipulate or promise employment to those recruited as associate probation officers.

They have also had volunteers who worked full-time as corrections and law enforcement officers. Many successful volunteer probation officers have a background in counseling.

Orange County has a 70-hour basic training stint, which runs seven weeks for two nights per week and a

Saturday session. On-the-job training takes around five weeks with a family filled graduation that follows.

The impressively large number of auxiliary probation officers in the Memphis/Shelby County endeavor start off with a 27-hour basic training course. The nine classes, which runs three hours apiece, are held three weeknights a month for three months.

Thomas Sunday and his wife have taken that training and their personal commitment to the streets of Memphis where they make a difference in people's lives.

Concluded dedicated auxiliary probation officer Thomas Sunday: "This is our nation's future. We have to do this."

Dr. Richard Weinblatt

January 2000
Law and Order:
The Magazine for Police Management

Volunteers Assist in Private/Public Sector Partnership

Mike Webb and Alan Smith cruised down Highway 74, outside of Charlotte, North Carolina, their radar picking out errant speeding truckers. In their white four door Chevrolet Lumina and black BDU style uniforms, the two look like members of an elite law enforcement group. In a way, they are.

The North Carolina Transportation Association, a private trade group comprised of 850 member companies, has stepped efforts to clean up the trucking industry's image regarding safety and accidents. The group, which has counterparts nationwide, has 50 designated safety officers under its self-supported Safety Management Council umbrella. Around 19 of that number are active on road safety patrol.

Other activities include public and law enforcement training endeavors geared towards drug interdiction, commercial vehicle inspection and accident investigation.

The various states have different emphasis areas depending on problems in their locales. Among the topics other states concentrate on are cargo theft and public outreach. Webb said the emphasis in North Carolina has been working with local officers to train them and make it feasible for those in smaller jurisdictions to dedicate more resources to truck safety inspection and enforcement.

For the most part, the safety team members have full-time occupations as safety executives with rucking concerns. The member companies provide the safety teams with paid time and equipment as part of the industry's effort to police their own.

They also teach local law enforcement officers the ins and outs of trucking. Many of the safety officers go beyond normal company compensation levels and, in effect, donate the time. Webb usually dedicates three days per month to his safety team duties.

Webb, who is the corporate fleet manager responsible for safety and compliance for Family Dollar Stores Trucking, said it was crucial for the trucking industry to provide assistance to local police in the form of expertise and grants. "North Carolina ranks sixth in the nation in truck related fatalities," reported Webb who patrols the counties of Union and Mecklenberg, NC. "The trucks are getting bigger and faster and the roads are getting smaller."

Safety officers who participate in the voluntary program have at least five years of truck industry experience. Many have extensive accident investigation and commercial vehicle inspection backgrounds.

Safety Patrol

The highest profile aspect of the safety officers' work is the road safety patrol jaunts. Webb's Lumina, like the other corporate vehicles used for the endeavor, is an antennae laden four door sedan loaded with $5,000 worth of scanners, Doppler radar, strobe lights, and a laptop computer that can download on-board truck data. Webb and his colleagues have their own radio frequency, which goes through a repeater based in Charlotte, NC. Safety Officer magnetic logos are sometimes affixed to the vehicles to further highlight their efforts.

While on patrol, safety officers look for trucks speeding, tailgating, or having faulty equipment. The officers send a form reporting the violation to the offending trucking company. The safety officer's identity is protected via the use of a protected ID number.

"That piece of paper carries a lot of weight for drivers as it gets their carrier's attention," said Smith who has spent 21 years in the trucking field. The field-based observations give the safety officers an idea of which carriers may habitually speed or may be involved in accidents.

The safety officers also occasionally leave the privately owned vehicles to team up with state, county and municipal law enforcement officers in their official patrol cars. The presence of safety officers is a factor in providing a one on one truck oriented educational experience for the sworn officers.

As representatives of the private trucking industry group, the safety team members do not have the authority to stop offending drivers. Teaming them with sworn personnel provides occupational trucking expertise to the people empowered to make the traffic stops.

Education

While primarily geared towards law enforcement, the safety team members do go into public schools and educate students regarding trucks. Some also teach defensive driving courses to driver education students.

"Some trucking firms get unsatisfactory ratings from the Federal Highway Safety Administration and we'll go on site and work with the carrier to get their operation back in compliance," Webb said. He pointed out that the safety teams sometimes tackle the trucking companies on their own turf—the corporate parking lot.

Webb, who acts as the Safety Management Council's coordinator for the Drug Interdiction Assistance Program (DIAP), said that his group assists non-DMV agencies in obtaining grants to tackle drug smuggling via trucks.

"We know trucks inside and out. Many local officers do not look closely at trucks as smuggling tools because of a lack of knowledge of the required paperwork and hiding methods. We address those gaps in knowledge," Smith said.

In line with their educational and training push, the Safety Management Council provides commercial vehicle drug interdiction instructors for both a short three-day class and a longer week and a half session.

Webb said that they have a law enforcement relations committee to motivate non-DMV agencies to get involved in commercial vehicle enforcement. With trucks involved in a large percentage of collisions on the highways, Webb maintained that more police officers versed in commercial vehicle inspection would impact the problem.

The North Carolina group even works "joint station details" with neighboring states by brokering mutual aid pacts. The safety teams encourage law enforcers with the North Carolina DMV to team up with their counterpart officials from Virginia, Tennessee, and Georgia to weigh and inspect commercial trucks.

The private sector version of reserve truck troopers is driving forth on new roadways, creating a true private/public partnership that adds a much needed resource for law enforcement.

Dr. Richard Weinblatt

May 2001
Law and Order:
The Magazine for Police Management

Alaska's Reserves Brave the Elements

Police reserves in the remote city of Kotzebue, AK, operate in 80 below zero temperatures and 40 inches of snowfall. The frigid weather requires that police vehicles run 24 hours a day, seven days a week. Kotzebue Sound is frozen for more than half the year.

"The chill factor makes it hard," acknowledged Kotzebue Police Chief Greg Russell. Like many law enforcement executives, Chief Russell has had to come up with creative solutions to policing problems-volunteer personnel were the answer. He has ten full-time officers, ten corrections officers, and three reserves who serve a population of 3,600 located 33 miles north of the Arctic Circle on the western coast of Alaska. The only assistance that the officers of remotely located Kotzebue have is the Alaska State Troopers, whose 240 commissioned personnel are spread thin over a whopping 586,412 square miles. Reserve officers in Kotzebue make up an additional uniformed presence that would not otherwise be there.

"With our unique law enforcement situation here in Kotzebue, the reserves have a large impact," said Russell, whose agency fields around 7,000 calls for service a year.

Also utilizing reserves as part of the delivery of law enforcement services in Alaska is the Wasilla Police Department located 43 miles north of Anchorage. Chief Charlie Fannon, a former police chief in Haines, AK, and ex-deputy sheriff in Idaho, is a huge proponent of the reserve concept and has a very active program with nine reserves currently supporting 17 full-time Wasilla police officers.

"It costs us $69,000 a year in wages and benefits for a full-time officer. From May 199 to May 2000, the Wasilla reserves donated 3,361 total hours. That's over $100,000 in police manpower on the city's streets," said Fannon. The reserves must serve 12 hours a month on the road and are active on foot patrol, bike patrol, handicapped parking patrol and riding as a second officer with full-time officers.

Russell said that his reserves provide vital backup to his agency, which only has two or three full-time officers out at peak times. Kotzebue officers patrol the city, which encompasses 17,000 square acres in four wheelers and snow machines. The department houses the largest contract jail site in Alaska: a 38,000 square mile jail catchment area and 1,189 prisoners.

Kotzebue does not have a juvenile detention facility and officers had been previously unable to hold juveniles for offenses. Russell enlisted the reserves and paid them $15 an hour to sit with the juveniles overnight. "When they realized that they would be held overnight so that we could pull them out of the village the next day for arraignment, a lot of problems stopped," said Russell.

Fannon believes that the Wasilla reserve officers are his ambassadors to the community. The reserves' full-time occupations bring them into contact with civilians in a way that full-time officers do not.

Training

Alaska's Police Standards Council regulates minimum training for the full-time law enforcement officers in the state. Any training for reserve personnel is left up to the local police department, causing liability issues that force some departments to shy away from using reserve officers.

Kotzebue's Russell has a three phase training program in place that is built around information out of the state's police certification manual. The training starts with qualifying at the range, and then goes to wearing a uniform on patrol with a full-time officer and finally having police powers while on duty. Russell said that all officers, reserve and full-time, short quarterly and qualify twice per annum no matter what the weather conditions.

In addition to the 12 road hours, reserves in Wasilla attend a two hour advanced training session every Thursday night. Fannon sponsors reserve officers interested in furthering their training and he has sent them out of the city for high speed pursuit driving, control tactics, pepper spray, and ASP expandable baton sessions.

Even more impressive is the basic training philosophy that Fannon has. He sends the reserves to the full 21-week police academy regiment. "It's quite a commitment, but for someone who wants to get into the field, it's a good investment," said Fannon. Reserves can commute daily to the Anchorage Police Academy or stay at the residential Alaska State Trooper Academy in Sitka, AK.

"After seeing them complete the training, which is quite a commitment, and ride on patrol, they become a known quantity. This is a lot better than word of mouth," observed Fannon who hired two former reserves In January and said others have been picked up by Cordova Police, Anchorage Police and Ted Stevens International Airport Police in Anchorage.

Fannon said it is hard to hire full-time officers. In Alaska, only 2.5 are hired for every 100 full-time position applicants and Anchorage Police are even more selective at just 1.5 per 100. Reserve officers who have received police academy training provide a valid pool from which chiefs can recruit.

Fannon sees reserve service as a way for police administrators to weed out potential problem officers. "I hate to sound cold and heartless, but we're talking about people who can use deadly force and a liability to the city in the lawsuit happy society we live in," said Fannon. "That being said, I'll stack up the quality of officers in the Wasilla reserve program with any I've seen elsewhere. They are the best."

November 22, 2005
Officer.com

The Original Homeland Security Force: For volunteer cops, it's the same old 'thang'

You'll never guess who really is the original "homeland security" protection force. Go ahead, try to guess. Long before homeland security became the new catch phrase and the latest law enforcement trend, citizen officers volunteered with little fanfare. Their buzzword was "reserves."

For a decade, I authored a column called "Reserve Reports" for Law and Order: The Magazine for Police Management. Some of the columns published years ago highlight my position that the non-compensated pioneers in police and sheriff's agencies across the nation long ago pioneered the homeland security trail. Some of the old column titles tell the story even back then: "Beyond Hurricanes: Riots, Bombings are 21st Century Reserve Duties" (in the May 2000 issue) and

"Discovering a Valuable Asset: Reserve Search and Rescue Units" (from the May 1999 edition).

Known variously as reserve, auxiliary, special, and host of other names, volunteer officers have run the gamut in terms of their "hiring" agency's screening, training and deployment philosophy (ranging from unarmed "eyes and ears" with a distinctly different uniform to fully academy certified, armed sworn officer status). However, one concept has remained constant no matter how a law enforcement organization chooses to utilize their reserves: they all involve citizens looking to protect their neighbors from threats to the country.

Certain areas of the country have embraced the reserve concept wholeheartedly. Places like California, Florida, and North Carolina have ramped up the screening and training to mirror the standards applied to their full-time counterparts. Others, such as Delaware, have backed away from the volunteer officer role.

There are quite a few examples out there that reflect a direct involvement in stereotypical homeland security efforts. In Vermont (one of only a half dozen states that use non-full-time troopers), armed auxiliary state troopers help with border issues in their 27 patrol boats, 30 snowmobiles and four ATVs. Auxiliary troopers in the marine unit patrol Lake Champlain.

Such obvious homeland security related duties are not just restricted to the United States. In Canada, auxiliary constables attached to the British Columbia unit of the Royal Canadian Mounted Police (RCMP) participate in programs such as Coastal Watch and Airport Watch. Like many agencies, the RCMP are concerned with stretched resources in the face of policing demands.

One of my colleagues in the small world of reserve law enforcement research underscores my contention that the new community volunteers are really related to the old citizen-based initiatives of years gone by. In his recent book, <u>Citizens Defending America: From Colonial Times to the Age of Terrorism</u> (University of Pittsburg Press), Dr. Martin Greenberg quite accurately frames the historical context of reserve type involvement.

"Citizens helping the police to protect the neighborhood, especially when the nation is under attack, is not new," opined Brooke Webster, the president of the Reserve Police Officers Association (RPOA), whose aunt was an aircraft spotter during World War II. "When all the career police officers went to war, much of the law and order was maintained by reserve types."

Webster's rendition of history is correct. The RPOA's website's history page is full of citizen-based policing examples. Reserves have evolved over the years. Spurred partly by liability concerns, reserve policing has grown in sophistication from the simplicity of the night watch with its hue and cry and the ruggedness of the frontier posse.

Any honest look at the history and current state of reserves reveals that they have become steeped in controversy and are looked down upon by full-time officers in some agencies. While there are a host of reasons for the animosity (I'll examine some of them in future "Reserve Power" columns), most law enforcers should agree that the priority of homeland security in the police mission is best accomplished with the help of dedicated citizens.

Nowhere has the impact of homeland security mandates been felt more than in smaller, rural agencies. Strapped for manpower, they have turned to reservists. Rural departments from West to East have tested this theory out in the real world.

Tim Dees, Officer.com's editor, found this out a few years ago first-hand when he oversaw training for the State of Oregon in an area that encompassed vast stretches. As he relayed to me, "The departments were very small and reserve officers were essential to getting the job done."

Dees, a former full-time police officer in Reno, Nevada, correctly found that rural areas rely even more than urbanized locales for reserve support in the protection of the populace. "In many cases it was a question of being able to get an officer there at all."

That's not a recent development. In a March-April 1997 Sheriff Magazine article I wrote, "Sheriffs Take on Rural Patrol Challenge," I cited several counties with far-flung population centers that utilize reserves. Alabama's Shelby County and Santa Fe County, New Mexico, use reserve deputies to extend the reach of the agency. In California, the San Bernardino County Sheriff's reserves staff everything from patrol units to search and rescue in one of the larger programs in the U.S.

Reserves, then as now, are the hidden weapon in the homeland security force. Recruited, screened, trained, and deployed in a quality-driven manner, reserve officers can be a powerful addition to a law enforcement agency's arsenal. They've been doing long before homeland security became the latest law enforcement trend. I expect they'll continue in their original role.

January 2, 2006
Officer.com

The Ultimate Sacrifice: Line of Duty Deaths Underscore Officers' Service

Reserve Officer Russell Simpson was part of a group of officials in Bandon, Oregon, attempting to rescue a thirteen-year-old boy from the ocean surf. The 51-year-old had served as a reserve for four years with the small, but close-knit Bandon Police Department. The teen, along with others swept into the currents, were rescued on that fateful December day in 2003. All that is except for Simpson. Simpson was a retired firefighter with the Los Angeles County Fire Department in California and drowned during his efforts to save the teenager.

Auxiliary Trooper Edward W. Truelove's actions in November 1992 saved two lives but ended with his name etched on the Connecticut Police Chief's Memorial. Serving the Connecticut State Police on that tragic Friday night, Truelove, 73, directed the driver and passenger of a disabled automobile off of I-84 in Chesire, Connecticut, just moments before a truck driver rear-ended his marked cruiser.

Forsyth County, North Carolina, Sheriff's Department Reserve Sergeant James Milton Johnson Sr., 59, was shot after serving law enforcement in a variety of capacities for 35 years. Milton's actions confronting a gunman who had already shot and killed two people are believed to have saved the lives of his 10-year-old grandson and the murdered couple's five-year-old son. Johnson's son-in-law, a full-time deputy responded and both he and the suspect were wounded in the ensuing firefight.

In Washington, DC, Reserve Officer Joseph Pozell, 59, was directing traffic on May 14, 2005, in the Georgetown section of the district. A three-year-veteran of the Metropolitan Police, Pozell was struck by a vehicle and succumbed to his injuries three days later. What made the death even more tragic was the presence of thousands of law enforcers in the nation's capital for National Police Week.

Reserve officers, sometimes also known as auxiliaries or specials, serve in a variety of ways depending on the preferences of their jurisdiction. Some are armed, while others aren't. Some reserves have full police powers, while others are more restricted in their authority. What is a common denominator is that all are subject to serious injury and even death. The situations above are but a few illustrations of the many reserves that meet the same fate.

Often unseen, reserve officers have served alongside our nation's law enforcers and faced many of the same risks. They have also, unbeknownst to many people, made the ultimate sacrifice while in service to their neighbors. Families of reservists killed in the line of duty are often left as the only ones who remember the honorable service of their loved one.

Fortunately, there are a few organizations that have been trying to raise the profile of these officers and their ultimate sacrifice. They want the officers and their families to get the credit and recognition that they so rightfully deserve.

"Reserve officers play an important role and these deaths are reminders of the sacrifices they make," said Chris Cosgriff, chairman of the Officer Down Memorial Page, Inc. (ODMP), which has included reserve type officers on its webpage since its inception in January 1996.

"Reserve, auxiliary, or part-time does not enter into our selection process. We don't care about the pay status of the officer," said Cosgriff.

Craig W. Floyd, the well-known chairman of the National Law Enforcement Officer Memorial Fund (NLEOMF), also maintains a website that lists officers who have died in the line of duty. His organization also lists volunteer and part-time officers on their website, in addition to the National Law Enforcement Memorial wall located in Washington, DC.

"We had discussions early on regarding inclusion criteria," recalled Floyd. "This past year, we clarified the criteria to include railroad officers, campus police, military police, as well as less than full-time officers."

Floyd said that he and his staff look at the individual's job title, job description, training, and circumstances of death. They also look at the presence of powers of arrest. Cosgriff's website also uses the officer's service to the agency and powers of arrest as indicators for inclusion.

Finding the Officers

A check of the websites reveals quite a few officers that have made the ultimate sacrifice. However, even the people running the databases have trouble identifying all of the reserves and auxiliaries that have passed away as a result of their law enforcement role.

Both said that they rely extensively on the family and friends of the officers to notify them.

"Reserve officers and families of deceased officers give us quite a bit of feedback. They thank us for including them and say that they are sometimes overlooked in the profession," commented ODMP's Cosgriff.

Pinning down the numbers of non-full-timer officers that have been killed is not so simple. The numbers generated by ODMP and NLEOMF are, by their own admission, probably under the actual numbers.

"We work with the Reserve Police Officers Association to try to identify officers who should be added," said Cosgriff. He noted that the Reserve Police Officers Association also has a page on its website that lists officers.

The main way that all three of the listing organizations find out about these officers is by reading of an officer's death with his title reflecting the status. It is the same way that they search through their databases to identify non-full-timer officers who have been killed.

Not all departments actually title their volunteer or part-time personnel with "reserve" or "auxiliary." Numbers that are generated only reflect those with easily identifiable titles such as reserve and auxiliary.

The term special officer transcends the stereotypical reserve role in many cases and the organizations were not sure if the title search for special officer would be a true reflection of the topic of this column.

By the Numbers

NLEOMF's Floyd and his staff searched and found that 43 non-full-time officers are listed in their database as having lost their life in the line of duty. The reserve title was borne by 24 and the remaining 19 utilized the term auxiliary.

In response to the research request, the NLEOMF also found 21 officers that had the word "special" in their title. Floyd was hesitant to include those 21 as non-full-time officers as their true status was unclear. Many specials are actually employed full-time.

"The term special generally has two meanings," said Cosgriff." "The first being equivalent to a reserve or auxiliary officer. The other being that the officer holds a police commission, and works full-time, but is not an official member of a town/city police department."

Cosgriff explained further by noting that the last special officer killed, Special Officer Dwayne Reeves, "held a police commission through the Newark (NJ) Police Department, but was actually employed by the Newark School District."

Cosgriff's search through their database found 81 with the title reserve and 35 who had auxiliary in their rank for a total of 116. Another 106 were classified under special.

Looking at these statistics can be depressing, however information to help other officers may be gleaned from reading the profiles on the websites.

Floyd pointed out that the numbers for full-time officer deaths are starting to fall.

Important Lessons

"There has been a 36% decline in shooting deaths," said Floyd who attributed the drop to better officer training, the wearing of bulletproof vests, and the nationwide drop in violent crime. But he also noted a 40% increase in traffic related deaths.

Floyd said this should especially be a concern for reserves, as well as the law enforcement executives who oversee reserve programs. Reserves and auxiliaries in all departments, even those in which they play a limited role, do handle traffic related duties.

"More than half the full-time officers are shot to death, but only one third (of the 43 reserve and auxiliary officers in the NLEOMF database) were shot. The vast majority of reserve and auxiliary officers were killed in traffic related functions," said Floyd.

The sobering statistic underscores the need for managers of non-full-time law enforcement personnel to ensure that proper equipment is issued and training is done.

"They (reserves and auxiliaries) need higher visibility clothing and they should be trained to be extra careful at accident scenes," observed Floyd after analyzing the numbers.

The deaths of reserve law enforcers are often unnoticed by all but their families and loved ones. These three organizations, and their websites, are striving to give recognition to those who made the ultimate sacrifice in service to their neighbors. That selfless act is perhaps the most important lesson to be learned.

Dr. Richard Weinblatt

Dr. Richard Weinblatt

February 6, 2006
Officer.com

Why Some Cops Hate Reserves: A crack in the police family

We've all heard the names at one time or another: "rent-a-cop," "wannabe," "2.5," as well as a host of other derogatory terms. There has long been a sense of friction between reserve and full-time officers in many departments. That animosity rises to the level of hate and is more pronounced in certain regions of the country. This "Reserve Power" column examines why such negativity abounds.

Some of the negativity is just downright mean-spirited and emanates unreasonably from a faction of officers in many departments. However, some of the problems could be curtailed if certain details are attended to in the reserve program. In my experience on all sides of the reserve fence (as a reserve, a full-time officer/reserve liaison, and as a police chief having formed a reserve officer program), it appears that the dislike comes from several different areas.

Political appointees

Law enforcers across the country, with their low tolerance for things that do not seem quite right, withdraw their informal support when reserves find their way to a badge and gun on a political basis. While political appointees are not bad in and of themselves (they can be a powerful advocate for the chief or sheriff with certain key constituencies), the swearing in of those individuals that could not otherwise meet the entrance and training standards irks full-time officers.

Officers view themselves as an elite cadre of professionals and resent those who enter their domain without the proper "ticket of admission."

Low standards

Related to the first category, reserve type officers that are appointed while not meeting the high standards applied to full-timers, isolates the reserve group. Officers look to other officers as their lifeline in times of trouble. Full-timers need the reassurance of equivalent standards for entry and training in their reserve backup force.

Entrance standards should reflect those applied to full-timers. Anything less encourages the derisive "wannabe" label as "those officers are of a class that could make it through the full-time standards." Even if the individual could meet those rigorous standards but chooses not to due to economic and career choices, the lack of those standards being applied to the reserve paints him or her as not measuring up.

On the training front, an agency truly committed to the reserve concept, should, while not lowering their standards, make it easier for those interested in serving their community to achieve the benchmark. For example, basic academy training should be scheduled in a manner that meets the needs of most working adults.

Separation

Sometimes, organizational structure can contribute to the discord. Departments that isolate their reserve contingent further widen the chasm that exists between reservists and full-time officers. Reserves are often relegated to the bowels of the agency (such as the basement) and are not integrated into the patrol shifts. Engaging in separate briefings and patrol stints from the regulars neither provides a learning nor collaborative environment for reserves or full-timers.

Going even a step further, an organizational chart that places the reserve operation far away from the patrol branch of the agency, traditionally the place where most reserve activity occurs, isolates the volunteer badge carriers.

I often saw, particularly in the Northeast, volunteers referred to as an "officer" in the "auxiliary police" instead of as an "auxiliary officer" in the "police department." The former distances the auxiliary officer, while the latter fosters a department-wide inclusive approach.

Distinctive uniforms

Beyond the officer safety issue, differentiated uniform and vehicle markings widen the schism between the two types of law enforcers. Officers view their reserves as being less of an officer and that perception is reinforced by the differentiated appearance.

Many departments have told me over the years of instances where reserves were specifically targeted by protesters and others with the thought that it would be easier to get them angry than a regular officer. The distinctive uniform made that focus possible. A few departments even changed the uniforms to more closely or identically resemble the full-timers' version as a result of undue problematic attention to their reserve personnel.

Rank insignia

Speaking of uniforms, many officers I have spoken to over the years looked down on the presence of rank insignia on reserve officers. While a chain of command and supervisory positions within a reserve group is good, the visible ranks confuse the public and cause resentment on the part of full-timers.

Both full-time and reserve officers have reported to me the confusion that occurs on a scene when, for example, a reserve captain pulls up and the citizen leaves the primary officer to go talk to "the boss." Worse yet, some civilians have been known to register complaints on officers with the gold laden reserve that arrives on scene.

Some departments, particularly larger ones where many officers do not know each other personally, delineate reserve rank by using unobtrusive uniform insignia such as colored bands on the epaulet or a different serial number on the badge

Fear of job encroachment

In many agencies, particularly those that do not have a lot of calls for police service, salaried officers fear that reserves may encroach of their tasks and thus jeopardize their jobs. While this fear is usually unfounded, there have been cases where governmental entities have misused their reserve programs. In a short-sighted move, they have used volunteer officers to replace full-timers. This is contrary to the concept of reserves which is to augment regular personnel.

Unfortunately, as so often is the case, the target of the officers' ire becomes the reserve that complies with an order, as opposed to the organization that issues the order. Thus the reserve becomes unfairly the brunt of the anger.

Regional differences

I have seen this to be the case particularly in agencies that have around a long time and have strong unions. The resentment of reserves seems particularly strong in the Northeast and Upper Midwest.

Some of the animosity is driven by the presence of unions and traditions steeped in the history of the departments' histories. On the other hand, reserves are more integrated and accepted in Western states and in the Southeast.

Interestingly, reserves in many of the states where acceptance by full-timers is highest have state standards or POST commissions that set equal or similar hiring and training standards for full-timers and reserves. Along the same lines, the reserves are equipped and deployed on a basis that mirrors their salaried counterparts.

With all of the people in society who do not have law enforcement officers on their Christmas card list, it seems silly to have fighting within the station house. The majority of the animosity rises out of misunderstandings and a less than sophisticated rollout of the reserve program. Reserves that are recruited, trained, and deployed in a professional manner should be a welcome addition to the police family. They should not be relegated to the role of black sheep of the family.

Dr. Richard Weinblatt

March 6, 2006
Officer.com

The Flip Side: Why Some Reserves Hate Cops

Last month's Reserve Power for Officer.com, "Why Some Cops Hate Reserves," was among the most read columns. I was inundated with emails (some rather lengthy) which underscored that the topic hit a nerve with both reservists and their full-time counterparts. This month's column explores the flip side: why some reserves hate the full-time officers they assist.

So often we hear of full-time officers who disdain reserves within their agency. Clearly, that struck a chord with this column's readers. What we hear of less often are the strong negative feelings that some reserves have towards the very officers that they are duty bound to assist.

Second Class Treatment

283

The main cause of much of the hard feelings is the lack of respect reserves and auxiliary type officers feel that some full-timers have for them. For a number of reserves, that treatment by a few officers translates into a broad-brush indictment of all salaried personnel.

While it is understandable in some individual cases, it is a mistake for reserves to lump all officers into the same category of "reserve-hater." Much as officers do not like it when a case of police misconduct results in a blanket condemnation of all law enforcers by the public, all officers should not be considered as anti-reserve.

Many reserves can understand the need for some reserve programs to utilize hand-me-down equipment. They can even go along with doing some less than glamorous duties to free up full-timers for more pressing needs. But what irks them the most is the lack of respect that they get from full-time officers.

Several emails I received lamented the fact that many officers disparage them without even getting to know them as individuals. The label "R" is almost seen (especially in some regions of the nation) as a scarlet letter.

While there are bad apples in every group (yes, even among the full-time ranks), the killer for reserves is how they are condemned as a group for the sins of a few. Every area has tales of reserves who overstepped their bounds or otherwise abused the trust bestowed upon them when they were handed their badge.

One needs only to look at David Berkowitz, the notorious son of Sam killer, who served as an auxiliary officer with the New York City Police Department, or serial killer John Wayne Gacy, who sported an Illinois deputy sheriff badge.

But the flip side does exist as well. At the extreme end of honorable service, many reserves have died doing their "hobby cop" (as derisively labeled by some) duties. As evidenced in my first Reserve Power column, "The Ultimate Sacrifice," reserves have long demonstrated their dedication to the officers and communities they serve by even laying down their lives in the line of duty.

The vast bulk of reserves serve in the in between little noticed area of good policing (much like most full-timers). While they don't generate a high profile or demand officers to be thanking them every minute, they also do not expect to be disrespected for doing their community service duty.

I am sad to say that many reserves in the United States walk into police services buildings where the full-timers turn their backs and ignore them. That kind of second-class treatment does not create a warm and fuzzy feeling on the part of reserves towards the law enforcement profession. As a result of such unprofessional treatment, I have seen reserves quit with a very sour taste in their mouths concerning the world of policing.

Silent Majority

While it varies from region to region and department to department, I believe that the majority of law enforcement officers appreciate the work of reserves. Many an officer, including your truly, served as a reserve prior to becoming a full-time law enforcement officer.

One would hope that these officers would stand up to defend individual reserves at the slightest hint of mistreatment. Sadly, in many cases they do not. I encourage full-timers to stand up and defend the good, hard-working reserves that are not being shown the proper respect.

In this age of community policing, reserves are the ultimate ambassadors to the neighborhood. As recruiters know, it is hard to find good officers and reserves. It does not make sense to run them off after they've been screened, trained and deployed.

As the last column mentioned, many problems stem from organizational issues concerning that screening, training, and deployment. Given that issues may be present in a given organization, it seems to be unprofessional to take that out on the reserves that are fulfilling the agency's mandate.

The silent majority needs to stand up and back up those reserves that are truly a help to, and a part of, the law enforcement family. There are enough people out there that dislike law enforcers for there to be hatred in the family.

April 21, 2011
PoliceReserveOfficer.com

Why Police Reserves Are So Important

So why does service as a reserve or auxiliary police officer make sense for the individual, law enforcement entities, and the community? What could possibly be the justification for putting people in harm's way often for strangers? Why would they go through that POLICE LINE DO NOT CROSS in the picture to the left? Really, why would someone cross over that protective police crime scene line?

Times are tough. Reserves help fiscally strapped governments do more with tax dollars and assist full-timers who otherwise would be unaided.

Full-time police job competition is fierce. Service as a police reserve officer allows for the gaining of valuable training, certifications, and experience.

Better screening of applicants for full-time police officer and deputy sheriff slots. From the law enforcement agency's perspective, it allows them to see the reservist in action. They have an established track record that places the aspiring full-timer head and shoulders above many other applicants. If you were a police chief or sheriff, who would you trust to take a chance on- someone you know has a proven track record in uniform or someone who doesn't have that fantastic resume building experience and training? I think you know the answer.

Reserves are the ultimate in community policing. They put the police in the community and the community in the police. Your neighborhood banker, lawyer, teacher, student, firefighter, and practically every walk of life person who serves as a police reserve officer is embedded among the people in a way that no full-time law enforcement officer can. They are the biggest ambassadors and supporters for the department's programs and initiatives.

Reserves represent the finest in civic service. After the tragedy of 9/11, many people had their passion for service and civic pride awakened. Serving as a reserve officer serves our nation and makes the person part of a cause greater than them. They contribute their time, offer their expertise and training, risk their personal safety, and make a difference in the lives of others.

In addition to the tangible benefits for aspiring police officers, community activists, and the departments, the bigger picture sees the benefits of reserves too. On top of valuable experience, training, and credentials, serving as a police reserve officer is among the most important of callings. What are you waiting for?

April 22, 2011
PoliceReserveOfficer.com

Police Job Jumpstart: Police Reserves Standout

We've all seen this or maybe you are living it yourself. The endless nightmare of answering job announcements for police officer, deputy sheriff, or state trooper positions only to find you didn't make the cut. You took written tests, physical agility tests, went to oral boards, and so on.

So what can you do to get that coveted thumbs up on your quest to become a police officer? How do you get past all the hurdles? And trust me there are many hurdles. Some of those are you (I can't tell you much if you've abused cocaine for the last ten years or are a convicted child molester), while others deal with issues beyond your control (such as government budget cuts).

It's frustrating and it's only getting harder as government tax revenues plummet and the stimulus money from the Obama administration fades in the memory. So what can you do to jump-start your law enforcement career? How can you get that chance to over the hordes of other aspiring law enforcers?

Service as a volunteer or part-time paid officer, referred to by various titles such as reserve, auxiliary, or special, is something that will make your application stand out from the pack. As a police chief, I would look at stacks and stacks of applications from people just like yourself to wanted to pin on that badge and feel the pride of serving as a law enforcement professional.

One of the reasons I was able to become a police chief, criminal justice professor, police academy director/instructor, etc. was due to my serving as a law enforcement reservist. I remember the roots of my career fondly and acknowledge its contribution to my life. It kept my career going forward for a number of reasons.

1. Screening. While the screening varies from location to location (depending on state and local rules), the process to become a police reserve officer is identical or closely mirrors that of the full-timers. Folks who want to become a police reserve officer have to go through a testing process that may include all the components used to process the full-time counterparts. That could include written and physical agility testing, interviews, and psychological and medical examinations. This is good experience for you

and puts you in a different league if a full-time slot opens up later.

2. Training. Again, depending on where you will serve, police and sheriff's reserves have to undergo the same or similar level of training as full-time sworn personnel. In states like Arizona and North Carolina, there is only one level of law enforcer and that is a fully trained and certified person. The state requires the training certification and does not care if the local agency pays the officer or deputy sheriff all the time, part of the time, or none of the time (volunteer). That training at the Police Academy includes firearms, community relations, and all the other usual stuff. The agency looking to hire someone in a full-time slot will favor the reserve, if not officially than unofficially, since the state certified and trained officer can step into the full-time slot with little or no more cost in training. In a fiscally conservative atmosphere of government now, this appeals to police chiefs, sheriffs, and their administrative staff.

3. Experience. Working as a police reserve officer gets you valuable experience that can't be gained from a book or in a classroom. You get to work under all sorts of conditions and you (and they) get to see how you like and can handle it.

4. Contacts. Working as a police reserve officer puts you in contact with in many cases the very people who decide who gets hired as full-time

officers. Do a good job, and they may want to bring you on as a salaried badge bearer. Of course the flip side is true too. Do a bad job, and it's easy to get rid of reserve type personnel and not hire them full-time either.

With all that training, experience, and contacts you developed as a police reserve officer, you have grabbed a hold of a valuable set of tools that you can use to jumpstart your law enforcement career. That's something that few others will bring to the table and allows you to stand out from the crowd. Go ahead, jumpstart your police career.

May 4, 2011
PoliceReserveOfficer.com

Police Reserves on The Cop Doc Radio Show

Police Reserve Officers are the featured topic discussing why they go down that dark, scary alley for free on The Cop Doc Radio Show on Thursday, May 5, 2011 at 7:00 pm eastern time. Hosted by police expert former police chief Dr. Richard Weinblatt, The Cop Doc, the show has featured a myriad of arresting guests and topics on police, crime, and safety issues.

Law enforcement reserves are also known by other titles including auxiliary, special, supernumerary, and intermittent depending on local rules and preferences. They serve on a volunteer or part-time basis for police departments and sheriff's offices across the United States and in other countries.

Quite often their work entails them going down those alleys that most people would dread. As will be described in the show: Imagine going down there as a police officer or deputy sheriff. Now imagine going down there for free.

On the expert panel for the show on volunteer and part-time law enforcement officers will be Florida Highway Patrol Auxiliary lieutenant colonel (ret.) and Volunteer Law Enforcement Officer Alliance (VLEOA) president David Rayburn, Orange County, FL, Sheriff's Office Reserve chief Tom Harrier, and Framingham Police Auxiliary captain and VLEOA director Marc Spigel.

The hour long show will cover why reserves risk their lives for little or no money, relationships between reserve and full-time officers, as well as issues of recruitment, screening, training, certification, deployment, and uniforming, as well as arming of reservists.

Listen to the show live on Thursday May 5, 2011 at 7 pm EDT at: http://www.blogtalkradio.com/the-cop-doc/2011/05/05/thecopdoc-police-reserve-officer.

Listen to the archived version or download the program at your convenience at the showpage link or from platforms such as podcasts from Apple iTunes, as well as Google-Listen, AppleCoreMedia, and PodTrapper.

There is usually a fairly active chat room and callers have called in from as far as Japan and England. The Cop Doc Radio Show call in number is (646) 652-4259.

May 17, 2011
PoliceReserveOfficer.com

Police Job Applicants Arrested: Sex, Drugs, and Jail

Whether you are a full-time or reserve police officer or deputy sheriff job applicant, this cautionary tale is for you. A recent story out of California about a San Diego Police job application and its jail bound author reminded me of the wide variety of folks that inexplicably apply to become a law enforcement officer.

Many do not deserve to make it through the process. Thankfully usually, honorable police executives do their best to weed people out that have no business being placed in a position of public trust.

According to published reports, Robert Williams admitted on the questionnaire to have had sexual contact with a child, as well as having viewed child pornography. As a former police chief and police academy director, I have long advised aspiring reserve and full-time law enforcers to be honest and forthright in answering all questions in the police hiring process. Of course, any omissions in our business are also considered a lie.

And so, here is San Diego Police officer candidate Robert Williams who gets busted for what is apparently a track record of abhorrent sex crimes involving children. Search warrant results, along with statements from his others, helped to seal his being charged.

It is amazing that he would put himself in that place. Before anyone misreads that statement, I am not commenting on his honesty. I guess I should commend it (though it does seem a tad bit stupid – forgetting that he should not have done the crime to begin with). Rather, my head shaking stems from the fact that someone with this sort of alleged activity would think that they would be police officer material.

Before you think that this is unusual, a couple of other police applicant arrested stories…

Here's a story that I have shared with police academy cadets eager for their chance to pin on the coveted badge. A few years back, a young man sat down in front of a Las Vegas Metropolitan Police Department oral review panel in Nevada. Admitting honorably that he was nervous as the interview board went about their questioning, things seem initially to be going well. Here is the basic jist of what transpired.

Interviewer: "When is the last time you smoked Marijuana?"

Applicant: "Before this interview. I was nervous, so I needed something to calm my nerves."

Interviewer: "Next."

Again, not the exception. I remember in one agency that worked for, I was in charge of some areas including ride-alongs for members of the community interested in law enforcement. Civilian ride-alongs, as is the policy with most law enforcement agencies, have to fill out and sign a liability waiver and undergo a cursory background check.

A young man who was a criminal justice major college student filled out the paperwork and application requesting the rife-along. He seemed sincere in his interests and stated that he wanted to go into law enforcement. I ran the usual checks and, as we say in the biz, got a "hit." for a warrant for misdemeanor FTA (Failure to Appear in court on a previous charge).

So, I called up this young man and told him to come down to the station as his ride-along was ready for him. He got that ride-along, only not in the front seat and it was a one way ride- to the county jail.

You would think that this serious young college student would have made sure that any warrant would be cleared up before pursuing his dream of being a cop. Of course, you'd also think that an accused pedophile would realize that those activities could conflict with becoming a police officer.

Dr. Richard Weinblatt

May 18, 2011
PoliceReserveOfficer.com

Florida Police Reserve & Auxiliary Certification: Are They OK?

As a former police chief who ran a basic criminal justice academy in Florida, I often get questions on how to become a Florida certified and trained reserve or auxiliary police officer. This article also covers how to become a full-time police officer or deputy sheriff. Florida has been one of the more progressive states in mandating training standards for folks who serve on a volunteer or part-time basis with police and sheriff's offices throughout the Sunshine State.

Among the state agencies that use volunteer cops are the Florida Highway Patrol (FHP) and the Florida Department of Environmental Protection (DEP). Municipal police department and county sheriff's offices have also long embraced the concept that is the ultimate in community policing as it puts the police in the community and the community in the police.

Varied State Standards & Titles

State certification and training standards vary greatly around the United States. Some states have little or no oversight over non-full-time officers or vastly differentiate the mandate. Other states have strong rules and in some cases, such as Arizona and North Carolina, require the same training as that expected of full-timers.

Titles also vary widely reflecting local preferences. Some of the names used for volunteer and part-time law enforcers around the country include reserve, auxiliary, special, supernumerary, and intermittent.

Florida Reserves & Auxiliaries: Differences

In Florida, reserves and auxiliaries are given two distinctly codified titles with divergent training mandates. Reserve police officers and deputy sheriffs, under 943 of the Florida statutes, are trained to the same level as that of their full-time, salaried counterparts. As a fully certified (trained and sworn in) law enforcer, the reserve and full-time law enforcement professional both have a minimum of 770 hours of basic law enforcement academy training at a Florida approved training facility. Most of them are housed within the community college system including the one I ran at Seminole Community College, located North of Orlando in Sanford, FL.

Once they pass the State Officer Certification Exam (SOCE) and are sworn in by a hiring agency, reserves in Florida, unless administratively restricted by their police chief or sheriff, have the same authority to carry firearms and enforce the law as a full-time law enforcer. They can carry firearms off duty. The training mandated by the Florida Criminal Justice Standards and Training Commission (CJSTC) and enforced by the Florida Department of Law Enforcement (FDLE) is the same whether the officer is paid all of the time, part of the time, or none of the time.

Auxiliaries in Florida have authority while on duty and under the supervision of a fully state certified law enforcer (reserve or full-time). This state mandate is subject to interpretation by local police chiefs and sheriffs. For example, the Florida Highway Patrol allows its auxiliary state troopers to use marked FHP cruisers solo as long as the supervision takes place via the radio.

Florida auxiliary officers, deputies, and troopers have a current minimum training mandate of 319 hours. Again, the training must be taken within an approved basic academy setting. It includes some of the same "high liability" (as it is called in Florida) courses taught to fully certified officers including 80 hours for firearms, 80 hours for defensive tactics, and 40 hours for first aid. The 48 hour vehicle operations course is open to local discretion and may be eliminated for a 271 hour total training requirement. Most include the vehicle operations component.

Florida State Screening Standards

Minimum screening standards for all criminal justice officers across the state of Florida are uniform. Local agencies are welcome to apply stricter criteria for hire, but may not lower the entrance hurdles. These are standards that apply to the hiring, as well as the acceptance into training programs in academies.

Pursuant to Florida Statute 943, all criminal justice sworn personnel (full-time, reserve, and auxiliary law enforcement, corrections, and corrections probation) must meet the base following base standards in order to be admitted into an approved criminal justice academy and to be eligible for hire (volunteer or paid):

1. High School diploma or GED for Law Enforcement or Corrections. Bachelor's degree for Corrections Probation
2. Citizen of the United States
3. Pass Florida Basic Abilities Test (FBAT/CJBAT)
4. As per Florida Statute 943.13 (4), no felony is allowed. That includes guilty, no contest (nolo contendre), conviction, and adjudication withheld.
5. No misdemeanor if a person pleads guilty, no contest, or is convicted of a misdemeanor crime involving perjury or false statement.
6. No dishonorable discharge from the armed forces of the United States.
7. Pass a Physical Exam

The Florida Department of Law Enforcement oversees and inspects the approved training academies for law enforcement, corrections, and corrections probation. Here is a list they keep up of State of Florida Criminal Justice Training Centers. The state agency also oversees the certification of criminal justice officers.

Are Florida training standards OK compared to most other states? I certainly think that the state has been progressive in its approach. The answer is yes.

Appendix

Partial Listing of Published Articles by
Dr. Richard Weinblatt

Examiner.com June 30, 2010
"Policing the Twilight, Drake and Justin Bieber beats"

Examiner.com June 30, 2010
"Why police should suspect missing Kyron Horman's stepmom"

Examiner.com June 27, 2010
"Police shift tactics at G20 Global Economic Summit in Toronto"

Examiner.com June 27, 2010
"Reality TV show cop Betsy Brantner Smith: women police have come far"

Examiner.com June 27, 2010
"Detroit Police: proud of crime stat. murder rate drop"

Examiner.com June 24, 2010
"Experts question Joran van der Sloot's police blame game"

PoliceLink.com June 11, 2010
"You're In Trouble: Now What?"

PoliceOne.com June 5, 2010
"Police to Professor: Making the Move to Academia"

PoliceLink.com May 28, 2010
"10 Ways to Generate Complaints on Patrol"

PoliceLink.com April 22, 2010
"10 Rules for Police Resumes"

PoliceLink.com April 6, 2010
"10 Tips for Ride-Alongs"

PoliceLink.com March 11, 2010
"10 Tricks for Picking the Right Department"

Newark Advocate (OH) & NewarkAdvocate.com
January 15, 2010
"Police Academy Students Pursuing their Dreams"

PoliceLink.com October 15, 2009
"The Bottom Line of Seat Belts for Law Enforcers"

PoliceLink.com October 1, 2009
"10 Domestic Violence Reminders for Veteran
Officers"

PoliceLink.com September 2009
"Ten Tips for On Target Academy Firearms Training"

PoliceOne.com August 25, 2009
Weinblatt's Tips column: "Top 10 social networking
tips for cops"

PoliceOne.com August 3, 2009

Weinblatt's Tip column: "There's a New Sheriff in this Media Town"

CNN AC360 Anderson Cooper blog (guest writer on Anderson Cooper's CNN.com blog) - July 30, 2009 "Gates, Crowley and The President: Calling it how I see it"

PoliceLink.com July 24, 2009 "Response to National Racial Debate: Gates, Crowley and the President"

PoliceLink.com January 2009 "Bad Credit, Bad Applicant"

Domestic Preparedness Journal September 10, 2008 "When Disaster Strikes: Gaining Peace of Mind"

PoliceLink.com August 25, 2008 "Professionalism: What Does Your Badge Stand For?"

PoliceOne.com August 22, 2008 Weinblatt's Tips column: "P1 Exclusive: What law enforcement can learn from the Caylee Anthony case"

PoliceLink.com August 2008 "Answering Common Oral Hiring Board Questions"

PoliceLink.com July 2008 "10 Tips for Mastering the Police Oral Board"

PoliceOne.com May 16, 2008

"National Police Week: Reflecting on our vulnerabilities"

PoliceLink.com April 2008
"Getting Serious About Joining the Force"

PoliceLink.com November 26, 2007
"Ten Tips for Dealing with the Opposite Sex"

PoliceLink.com November 20, 2007
"Surviving Your Prisoner Transport"

PoliceOne.com November 16, 2007
Weinblatt's Tips column: "10 Taser tips for LEOs"

PoliceLink.com October 30, 2007
"Promotions: The Courses That Count"

PoliceLink.com July 2, 2007
"So you wanna be a cop... First impressions count!"

PoliceOne.com April 20, 2007
Weinblatt's Tips column: "Tips for major incident media relations in the wake of the Virginia Tech shooting"

PoliceOne.com February 16, 2007
Weinblatt's Tips column: "10 tips for officers engaged in off-duty incidents"

PoliceOne.com March 6, 2006

Weinblatt's Tips column: "PoliceOne Exclusive: Domestic disturbance response: 10 tips for winning at these volatile calls"

Officer.com March 6, 2006
Reserve Power column: "The Flip Side: Why Some Reserves Hate Cops"

Officer.com February 17, 2006
Career Corner column: "How to Keep Your Boss Happy: How to acquire power in the agency"

Officer.com February 6, 2006
Reserve Power column: "Why Some Cops Hate Reserves: A crack in the police family"

PoliceOne.com January 16, 2006
The Police and the Press column: "Press releases: Used and abused"

Officer.com January 16, 2006
Career Corner column: "Inside the FBI National Academy: The FBI NA and Others are Key to Promotion"

PoliceOne.com January 4, 2006
Weinblatt's Tips column: "Police officer suicide prevention: Officers kill themselves at higher rate than general population"

PoliceOne.com January 3, 2006
Weinblatt's Tips column: "PoliceOne members respond"

Officer.com January 3, 2006
Reserve Power column: "The Ultimate Sacrifice: Line of Duty Deaths Underscore Officers' Service"

Officer.com December 16, 2005
Career Corner column: "Academic Jobs for the Cop: How to Land those Teaching Gigs"

PoliceOne.com December 14, 2005
Weinblatt's Tips column: "Creative cuffing for small-wristed subjects"

Officer.com November 22, 2005
Reserve Power column: "The Original Homeland Security Force: For volunteer cops, it's the same old 'thang'"

PoliceOne.com November 21, 2005
Weinblatt's Tips column: "10 tips for talking with kids"

PoliceOne.com November 10, 2005
Weinblatt's Tips column: "Searching for a clue"

PoliceOne.com November 10, 2005
Weinblatt's Tip column: "Death notifications: A tough police assignment"

PoliceOne.com November 10, 2005
Weinblatt's Tips column: "Carrying a knife: Officer safety and administrative considerations"

PoliceOne.com November 10, 2005
Weinblatt's Tips column: "10 ways to minimize complaints"

PoliceOne.com November 10, 2005
Weinblatt's Tip column: "Firearms training: train like you play"

PoliceOne.com November 10, 2005
Weinblatt's Tips column: "Crime scenes: stopping the evidence eradication gremlins"

PoliceOne.com October 26, 2005
Tip: "Returning DL can help avoid consent problems"

The Orlando Sentinel (daily newspaper Orlando, Florida) October 19, 2005
Editorial: "A rip in fabric that holds law enforcement together"

PoliceOne.com October 19, 2005
The Police and the Press column: "The absence of a police marketing mentality"

Officer.com October 19, 2005
Career Corner column: "The Good, the Bad, and the Ugly of Online College Degrees"

PoliceOne.com October 12, 2005
Officer Safety Tip: "Officer safety: It's not just an on-duty thing"

PoliceOne.com October 3, 2005
Training Tip: "AlcoSensor breath samples: How to tell if your subject is cooperating"

PoliceOne.com September 26, 2005
Officer Safety Tip: "The forgotten piece of equipment: handcuffs"

PoliceOne.com September 19, 2005
Officer Safety Tip & Training Tip: "Intersection safety for backup units"

PoliceOne.com August 30, 2005
The Police and the Press column: "Putting a human face on the police: Making an emotional connection"

PoliceOne.com May 24, 2005
The Police and the Press column: "P1 Exclusive: Ten Tips for Working with the Media"

PoliceOne.com April 4, 2005
The Police and the Press column: "How History Makes the Future of Police Media Relations Clearer"

PoliceOne.com April 28, 2004
The Police and the Press column: "The Image in the Mirror: The Enemy has a Face"

The Courier-Tribune (daily newspaper Asheboro, North Carolina) Friday, April 23, 2004 Guest Column: "Appreciation for a job well done"

American Police Beat April 2004

"How to give yourself a good shot at the job: Don't shoot yourself in the foot before you even get to the interview"

The Courier-Tribune (daily newspaper Asheboro, North Carolina) Sunday, January 4, 2004
Guest Column: "Understanding your partnership with your police"

Sheriff Magazine January-February 2003
"Sheriffs' Psychologists: The Ultimate Backup for the Progressive Sheriff's Office"

Law and Order: The Magazine for Police Management May 2001
"Alaska's Reserves Brave the Elements"

Law and Order: The Magazine for Police Management May 2000
"Departmental Gyms Become Fitness Rooms: Final Phase in a Holistic Fitness Approach"

Law and Order: The Magazine for Police Management May 2000
"Beyond Hurricanes: Riots, Bombings are 21st Century Reserve Duties"

Law and Order: The Magazine for Police Management April 2000
"Solving High Tech Crimes: Private and Public Sector Partnerships"

Corrections Technology Management Magazine
March/April 2000
"Role-Playing"

Law and Order: The Magazine for Police Management
February 2000
"Creative Funding Makes AEDs a Reality in Patrol
Cars"

Law and Order: The Magazine for Police Management
January 2000
"Volunteers Assist in Private/Public Sector Partnership

Law and Order: The Magazine for Police Management
December 1999
"The Paramilitary vs. Academic Training Debate"

Law and Order: The Magazine for Police Management
December 1999
"Managing Off-Duty Jobs: A Clear Policy Is The Key
To Success"

Corrections Technology and Management Magazine
November/December 1999
"So You Want To Be a Volunteer Probation Officer"

Law and Order: The Magazine for Police Management
November 1999
"Bridging Gaps in Assignments: Villa Park Fills in with
Auxiliary and Part-time Officers"

Law and Order: The Magazine for Police Management
October 1999
"IACP Conference 1999: Charlotte: The Queen City"

Law and Order: The Magazine for Police Management
October 1999
"Charlotte-Mecklenburg Police: 21st Century
Technology and Community Service"

Law and Order: The Magazine for Police Management
October 1999
"The Shifting Landscape of Chief Jobs: What's Changed
and How to Forge a Path"

Law and Order: The Magazine for Police Management
September 1999
"Agencies Look to Year 2000: Assess Y2K Options"

Law and Order: The Magazine for Police Management
September 1999
"Volunteer SPCA Officers: Working with Local Police
to Protect Animals"

Law and Order: The Magazine for Police Management
August 1999 "Special Report: New Training Concept:
New Police Training Philosophy: Adult Learning Model
on Verge of Nationwide Rollout"

Law and Order: The Magazine for Police Management
August 1999 "RCMP Takes Learning to the Streets"

Law and Order: The Magazine for Police Management
August 1999
"The Evolution of Police Footwear: It is the Era of Air Jordans and Bloodborne Pathogens"

Law and Order: The Magazine for Police Management
May 1999
"Discovering a Valuable Asset: Reserve Search and Rescue Units"

Corrections Technology Management Magazine
October 1998
"Come Fly With Me: Feds Take to the Air to Help Locals with Safe, Economical Inmate Moves"

Corrections Technology Management Magazine
May/June 1998
"Point-Counterpoint: Weighing in on Privatization"

Law and Order: The Magazine for Police Management
May 1998
"Changing the Corporate Culture: How One State Agency Took on the Challenge"

Corrections Technology Management Magazine March 1998
"Locals Get A Piece of the Action from Uncle Sam: Strapped Jails Turn Finances Around: Facilities Garner Federal Prisoners and Dollars"

Law and Order: The Magazine for Police Management
February 1998
"Reserve Expertise Makes Air Support A Reality"

Corrections Technology Management Magazine
February 1998
"Point-Counterpoint: Showdown in the Arizona Desert:
Maricopa County's Tent City Jail"

Law and Order: The Magazine for Police Management
December 1997
"Negative Perceptions Common: Regulars Question
Value of Reserves"

Police: The Law Enforcement Magazine October 1997
So You Wanna' Be a Police Chief: Aspiring to the Top
Rank of Law Enforcement Today Takes More
Experience, Training, Education, Skills, and Political
Savvy Than Ever Before"

Law and Order: The Magazine for Police Management
September 1997
"Academies Put Civilians in the Shotgun Seat: Law
Enforcement Takes Community Policing to the Next
Level"

American Police Beat June 1997
"Is The Grass Greener at the Aurora, Colorado Police
Department?"

Law and Order: The Magazine for Law Enforcement
Management June 1997
"Riding with Reserve FTOs: Field Training Programs
Vary in Different Departments for Reserve Officer
Recruits"

Sheriff Magazine March-April 1997
"Sheriffs Take on Rural Patrol Challenge"

Law and Order: The Magazine for Police Management
April 1997
"Special Report: Bicycles: More Than Just a Balancing
Act"

Law and Order: The Magazine for Police Management
April 1997
"Rank Insignia for Reserves: Debate Revolves Around
Public Perception and Officer Acceptance"

American Police Beat March 1997
"The Paychecks are High and So Is Morale"

Law and Order: The Magazine for Police Management
March 1997
"Special Report: S.W.A.T.: Counseling and Support for
S.W.A.T. Personnel"

Sheriff Magazine January-February 1997
"Sheriffs Find Innovative Solutions: Providing Jail
Medical Services with Limited Funds"

Law and Order: The Magazine for Police Management
December 1996
"Advice for Reserves: The Reserves' Legal Eagles and
Insurance Icons Weigh In"

Police: The Law Officer's Magazine October 1996
"Have Gun, Will Travel: Gaining Certification in the
New Frontier"

Law and Order: The Magazine for Police Management
September 1996
"Reserve Duties Vary in the Bay State: Massachusetts
Officers Wear Many Hats"

Law and Order: The Magazine for Police Management
April 1996
"Reserve Officers Man Boats: Turnover is Low for
Police on the 'Baywatch' Beat"

Law and Order: The Magazine for Police Management
March 1996
"Reserves Patrol on Bicycles: This New Breed is
Cutting a Wide Path as they Pedal Forth"

Law and Order: The Magazine for Police Management
November 1995
"Take-Home Cars for Reserves: Officer Effectiveness
and Community Presence Enhanced by Program"

Law and Order: The Magazine for Police Management
August 1995
"A Class Act: University Police Reserves Pass the Test
of Professionalism"

Law and Order: The Magazine for Police Management
April 1995
"N. Carolina Reserves Among Top Ranked: Volunteers
Find the Sweat and Hard Work are Worth It"

Law and Order: The Magazine for Police Management
February 1995
"P.E.P. Program: Part-Time Officer Training in Illinois"

Law and Order: The Magazine for Police Management
December 1994
"Liaison Officers: A Vital Link in a Reserve Operation"

Law and Order: The Magazine for Police Management
September 1994
"Oral Boards Go High-Tech"

Law and Order: The Magazine for Police Management
August 1994
"Police Footwear Meets the 'Reebok Generation'"

Law and Order: The Magazine for Police Management
August 1994
"Battle Dress Utility"

Law and Order: The Magazine for Police Management
June 1994
"Seasonal Reserves: Part-time Paid Personnel Fill in the Gaps"

Law and Order: The Magazine for Police Management
April 1994
"Reserves, Regulars and Regulators: How They Work Together in New Mexico"

The Narc Officer March/April 1994
"Reserve Heroes"

Law and Order: The Magazine for Police Management
February 1994
"Reserves Mount Up: Provide Services Otherwise Curtailed"

Law and Order: The Magazine for Police Management
December 1993
"Professionalism Reduces Liability: Trained Reserves
Make Positive Contribution"

Law and Order: The Magazine for Police Management
October 1993
"Reserves Excel in the Sunshine State: Training
Exceeds Standards"

Law and Order: The Magazine for Police Management
August 1993
"Reserve Data Available: New Book Provides
Everything You'll Want to Know"

Police: The Law Officer's Magazine July 1993
"Credence & Credibility: Training, Selection Standards,
and Liability Still Top The List of Concerns About
Reserve Officers. Increased Professionalism, However,
Has Brought Increased Respect"

Law and Order: The Magazine for Police Management
June 1993
"Reserve Motorcycles: A Positive Public Relations
Impact"

21st Century Policing Summer 1993
"Volunteer Officers and Community Policing"

Law and Order: The Magazine for Police Management
April 1993
"Reserve Detectives"

The F.O.P. Journal Spring/Summer 1993
"Reserve Policing: Stepping Stone to a Career"

Law and Order: The Magazine for Police Management
February 1993
"'Freelance' Reserves"

Law and Order: The Magazine for Police Management
December 1992
"Reserve Wildlife Officers: A Different Breed"

Law and Order: The Magazine for Police Management
October 1992
"Reserve K-9"

Law and Order: The Magazine for Police Management
August 1992
"The Thin Line Between Reserve and Full Time"

Law and Order: The Magazine for Police Management
April 1992
"Alabama Reserves Alive and Well"

Law and Order: The Magazine for Police Management
February 1992
"The Police and The Media"

Law and Order: The Magazine for Police Management
February 1992
"The Golden State of California Reserves"

Law and Order: The Magazine for Police Management
December 1991
"The Birth of a Volunteer Officer Program"

The Police Investigator October 1991
"Hostage Incidents: The Experts Respond"

Law and Order: The Magazine for Police Management
October 1991
"The State of the State Reserve Trooper"

Law and Order: The Magazine for Police Management
September 1991
"Accreditation: A Force Affecting Reserve Officers"

The TMPA Quarterly July 1991
"Texas Reserve Cops: The Lone Star State is Pioneering the Way"

The Narc Officer February 1991
"The Use of Reserve Officers in the War on Drugs"

The Reserve Law Officer 4th Quarter 1990
"Does TV Depict 'Real Life' Police Work?"

Dr. Richard Weinblatt

Made in the USA
Lexington, KY
23 June 2012